THE
HERB
COMPANION
COOKS

THE
HERB COMPANION
Cooks

Recipes from the First Five Years of the
Herb Companion Magazine

INTERWEAVE PRESS

Photography, Joe Coca
Design and production, Marc McCoy Owens
Cover design, Signorella Graphic Arts
Herb Chart, pp. 2–3, Robin Taylor Daugherty

 Interweave Press, Inc.
201 East Fourth Street
Loveland, Colorado 80537
USA

Library of Congress Cataloging-in-Publication Data
CIP applied for.

First printing: IWP—30M:894:QUE

Acknowledgements

Contributors to *The Herb Companion Cooks* include home cooks, professional chefs, caterers, magazine columnists, and cookbook authors. They share a deep interest in and knowledge of herbs (most grow their own) and keen palates. Their styles range from the best of fresh, wholesome home cooking to the leading edge of flavor exploration. We thank them for the creativity and care that they've invested in the recipes they share.

Lynn Alley cooks, teaches, and writes in Carlsbad, California. Her current work in progress is a book on all the good, old fashioned basics: homemade breads, butters, vinegars, pastas, pickles, and more.
Basic Pizza Dough, Basil Garlic Butter, Two Tomato and Three Basil Salad, Dill Burnet Butter, Fresh Herb Pizza, Herbs in Butter, Lemon Verbena Muffins, Pizza Niçoise, "Plain Tomato" Pizza Sauce, Red Wine Vinegar Marinade, Two-Cheese-and-Three-Basil Pizza

Barbara Bassett of Gualala, California is a particularly prolific author; she has seven books and more than three hundred magazine food articles to her credit.
Jalapeño Mustard, Tarragon Mustard, Whole-Grain Mustard

Susan Belsinger and **Carolyn Dille** sometimes work independently, as they have on a few of the recipes listed below, but we usually think of them as the "dynamic duo" that has coauthored *Herbs in the Kitchen, The Garlic Book, The Chile Pepper Book*, and coming up in 1995, *The Greens Book*. Their extensive travels in southern Europe, Morocco, and the American Southwest have inspired many of the collaborative efforts listed below. Susan lives in Brookeville, Maryland, and Carolyn, in San Jose, California.

Recipes by Susan Belsinger
Buttermilk Cream Scones with Lemon Balm, Cantaloupe Sorbet, Carrots with Horseradish, Coriander Tea Torte, Cranberry-Apple Jelly with Rosemary, Endive and Radicchio Salad with Blue Cheese, Fresh Fruit Tarts with Orange Mint, Frittata with Peas, New Potatoes, and Mint, Herb Vinaigrette, Herb Sauce with Roasted Chiles, Herb Crackers, Herb Garden Special Tea, Herbed Cream Cheese and Watercress Sandwiches, Herbed Red Pepper and Ricotta Envelopes, Lemon Balm Poppy Seed Tea Loaves, May Wine with Strawberries and Sweet Woodruff, Nectarine and Plum Cake with Bergamot, Orange and Coriander Salad, Pears Poached with Rosemary and Chestnut Whipped Cream, Savory Cheddar Spread with Sherry, Strawberry Rhubarb Cobbler, Thai-style Stir-fry, Toasted Coriander Seeds, Tomato and Cucumber Salad with Basil Flowers

Recipes by Carolyn Dille
A Mess of Spring Greens, Baked Apples with Savory, Borage Fritters with Capers, Bouquets Garnis, Cambodian Crepes, Chervil Purslane Soup with Lettuce, Chicken Saté with Peanut Sauce, Chiles en Escabeche with Oregano, Crab Soup with Lemongrass and Coconut, Dill Dressing, Dilled Chicken Pot Pie, Fava Bean Soup with Savory, Mint and Tomatillo Salsa, New Potatoes and Peas in Dill Sauce, Red and Green Chile Basil Butter, Risotto with Seafood and Dill, Rocket and Fraises de Bois Salad, Sage and Poblano Cheese, Savory Phyllo Triangles, Smoked Trout with Savory, Smoked Fish Salad with Dill Vinaigrette, Spring Herb Salad, Yellow Beef Curry, Zucchini Dill Pickles

Recipes by Susan Belsinger and Carolyn Dille
Braised Chicken with Mace and Tomatoes, Breadsticks with Black Pepper and Cheddar, Buttermilk Dressing with Herbs and Green Peppercorns, Jamaican-style Greens, Mulled Rosemary Wine and Black Tea, Parsnips with Nutmeg and Parmesan, Spicy Butter with Four Peppercorns, Stewed Sweet Peppers, Stuffed Mushrooms with Oregano, Tunisian-style Snapper, Vegetables a la Grecque

Avid gardener and food author **Gail Damerow** of Gainesboro, Tennessee, is author of *Ice Cream! The Whole Scoop* published by Glenbridge Publishing and editor of the bimonthly magazine *Rural Heritage*.
Basic Rose Hip Sorbet, Herbal Sorbet Basics, Herbed Lemon Sorbet

Ingrid Groff gardens, cooks, writes, and looks after her two children in New Hampshire.
Ricotta and Parsley Puffs

Bread's the thing for **Beth Hensperger** of Cupertino, California, whose popular catering business, Bread and Food, provided the impetus for a book titled, of course, *Bread*.
Crusty Provençal Herb Rolls, Homemade Herb Breads, Italian Ricotta and Parsley Braid, Rosemary and Oregano Focaccia, Tomato Basil Baguette, Walnut and Herb Batter Bread

Mary Herrick is The Jazz Cook of Fort Collins, Colorado, a catering and personal cooking service.

Brie Pinwheel, Cheddar, Sage, and Walnut Torta, Goat Cheese and Pepper Torta, Italian Pesto Cheese Torta

Madalene Hill and **Gwen Barclay** of Cleveland, Texas, are known all over the country for their cooking lectures and classes, and in the Texas hill country and beyond for the wonderful inn and herb business that they ran for many years. They are coauthors of *Southern Herb Gardening*.

A Simple Fresh Herb Liqueur, A Master Recipe for Cordial, Baked Polenta with Italian Sausage, Mushrooms, and Three Cheeses, Classic Lemon Curd, Delicious Poultry Blend, Fiery Jalapeño Pesto, Flavored Vinegars, Four Thieves Vinegar, Frango Guisado a moda de Maria Gloria, Fresh Herbal Oil Concentrate, Golden Saffron Rice, Hearty White Bean and Fall Greens Soup, Herbal Liqueurs, Herbal Cheese Stuffing, Holiday Seed Cake, Hungarian Szeged Goulash, Lemony Chile Vinegar, Mint Chimichurri, Mushroom Caviar Stuffing, Super Simple Squash with Sage, Sweet Thyme Vinegar Pie, Thunder of Zeus, Warm Cherry Tomato Surprise, White Chocolate and Pine Nut Mousse

Austin, Texas, gardener, cook, and author **Lucinda Hutson** brings a well-tempered enthusiasm for the hot and spicy to her recipes. She's the author of *The Herb Garden Cookbook*, and has written for *Bon Appetit* and other magazines.

Bloody Mary Mix, Confetti Corn Relish, Fabulous Fajita or Chicken Marinade with Cilantro, Citrus, and Gold Tequila, Frijoles Negros en Olla (Balck Beans in a Clay Pot), Festive Fruit Daiquiris, Queso Flameado (Spicy Broiled Cheese), Sassy Sangria

Karen Iacobbo of North Scituate, Rhode Island, is dedicated to bringing great flavor and good nutritional value to vegetarian cookery through her writing, lecturing, and regular radio program on the subject.

Herbal Bean Sausages

Suzanne Jonkers is a freelance food journalist in Denver, Colorado. She has been on the editorial and test kitchen staffs of *Better Homes and Gardens, Cuisine,* and other magazines.

Basil Parmesan Cheese Straws, Bourbon Rosemary Almonds, Curried Orange Pork Ragout with Broccoli, Herbed Yogurt Cheese, Italian Vegetable Ragout, Oxtail Ragout, Parmesan Sage Leaves, Seeded Sage and Cheddar Wafers, Tarragon Chicken Triangles, Veal Mushroom Ragout

Fox River, Illinois, is home to **Linda Fry Kenzle,** a writer, cook, and avid gardener.

Cheese Thumbprints, Rosemary Glazed Carrots, Herb Honey, Herb Honey Jelly

Linda Ligon is editor and publisher of *The Herb Companion*.

Basic Basil Pesto, Brandy Madeleines, Cheese-Potted Basil, Double Ginger Pumpkin Pie, Ginger Beer, Hearty Herb Blend, Herb Stuffed Oysters, Pepper Cream Soup, Root Beer

Sharon Lappin Lumsden of Champaign, Illinois, is not only an energetic writer and herb gardener, but a weaver as well. She's working on a book titled, *Green Byways: Garden Discoveries in the Great Lakes States*.

Preserving Herbs for Tea

Brigitte Mars is an herbalist and nutritional consultant in Boulder, Colorado. Her weekly radio spot features all manner of herb lore.

National Herb Week Tea

A passion for converting neglected land into verdant herb gardens consumes much of the time of **M.J. McCormick** of Sutton, West Virginia.

Creamy Tarragon Sauce, Hot Marinated Mushrooms, Tarragon Dressing, Tarragon-Mushroom Consomme

Portia Meares of Madison, Virginia, is captivated by the many roles of herbs in our lives: culinary, medicinal, spiritual. She's a founding member of the International Herb Association, and former editor and publisher of *The Business of Herbs*. Rosemary is one of her favorite herbs.

Chicken Rosemary

People around Berthoud, Colorado, know **Rusty Muller** as the apostle of good cooking with herbs. Her classes in breadmaking and vegetarian cooking always draw crowds, and her annual fall herb sale is in its third decade.

Green Bean Soup, Herbs with Beans—A Harmonious Marriage, Split Peas and Rice, Stewed Black Beans, Whole Wheat Onion & Herb Bread

Dan Nicklas is a chef with Coopersmith microbrewery in Fort Collins, Colorado; he has developed menus for several Colorado restaurants.

Winter Squash Herb Bread

Ellen Ogden is test kitchen manager at The Cook's Garden, a mail order seed company in Londonderry, Vermont, and coauthor (with her husband, Shepherd) of *The Cook's Garden*.

Boursin with Fino Verde Basil, Cinnamon Basil Custard, Purple Basil Pesto

Mary Peddie is the 1995 recipient of the International Herb Association's annual service award, and the founder of that organization. She also has been the driving force behind The Herb Peddlar in Washington, Kentucky, and of a wholesale herb nursery in Rutland, Kentucky.

Mary Parrot's Secret Rose Geranium Syrup

Dutch Mill Farm in Puyallup, Washington, is home to **Barbara Remington**, a director of the Pacific Herbal Institute. Lavender is one of Barbara's specialties.

Lavender Jelly

Author of *Condiments!* and *A Taste of the Tropics,* **Jay Solomon** is also owner and chef of Jay's Cafe at Clinton Hall in Ithaca, New York.

Herbal Citrus Scones, Herbal Crepe with Strawberries and Bananas, Island Roasted Chicken with Thyme Mustard Sauce, New York Strip Steak with Thyme and Rosemary Salsa, Pineapple and Thyme Grilled Orange Roughy, Plum-Nectarine Vinaigrette, Raspberry Mint Muffins, Raspberry Vinaigrette, The Ultimate Herbal Salad, Thyme and Scallion Corn Muffins, Warm Spring Salad with Thyme and Feta Vinaigrette

Linda Underhill is a food writer in Alfred, New York, and **Jean Nakjavani**, a gourmet cook in nearby Bradford, Pennsylvania.

Lovage Cordial, Lovage Umbrella, Loving Mary Cocktail

Kathleen S. Van Horn
Violet Ice Cream

Donna Wild of Loveland, Colorado, first became interested in herbs in Austin, Texas. She is a member of the Herb Society of America.

Mulling Spice Beetle

Growing herbs is only the beginning for **Christine Wittmann** of Alton, New Hampshire. She also writes and lectures about them, sells them, and creates medicinal preparations from them for people and their furry friends at her business, aptly named Cat's Cradle.

Dandelion Fritters, Herb Pie, Pottage of Herbs

Terri Pischoff Wuerthner makes her home in Santa Rosa, California, where she revels in the abundance of local herbs and fresh produce. Terri is author of *Food for Life: The Cancer Prevention Cookbook.*

Anise Baby Squash Orientale, Basil Polenta with Mushroom Sauce, Braised Chicken with Creamy Herb Sauce, Cauliflower with Lemon-tarragon Mayonnaise and Cheese Crust, Chicken Breasts with Herbs in Parchment, Chocolate Strawberry Tostadas, Corn Soup with Herb Cream, Crab Cakes de Provence, Fresh Sage Muffins, Garlic Orange Chicken, Garlic-Olive Oil Potatoes with Fresh Rosemary, Grilled Herbes de Provence Salmon Fillet Sandwiches, Herbed Chicken Breasts Caribbean, Lamb Roast with Herbes de Provence Crust, Lemon Basil Vermicelli, Marjoram Grilled Chicken Breasts with Dill-chive Sauce, Potato Herbes de Provence Soup with Buttered Leeks, Redfish with Herb Pesto and Cream Sauce, Roasted Chicken Breasts with Herb Leaves, Scallops and Prawns Grilled on a Bed of Cinnamon Basil, Spinach and Watercress Salad with Baked Herbes de Provence Chèvre, Vegetables and Linguini on a Bed of Arugula and Radicchio, White Beans with Herbes de Provence Cream

Lois Young has had a long association with the Herb Society of America, and is a cook and herbal craft designer. She lives in Toledo, Ohio.

Chicken-Melon-Mint Salad, Zucchini Madeleines, Cheese Twists

Table of Contents

$\mathscr{I}$ntroduction

Scan the cookbooks many of us grew up with—Betty Crocker, Fanny Farmer, *The Joy of Cooking*,—and you find herbs doled out, in their dried and possibly powdered state, by the half- and quarter-teaspoon. The admonition was never to use more than one or two in the same dish, and never to let them assert their flavors to the point of being recognizable.

Tastes change. Today we seek out intense and complex flavor experiences: raw garlic, flaming peppers, pestos that concentrate all the goodness of a summer herb garden in each bite. Today's adventurous cooks grow their own herbs, seeking out choice varieties, and use them fresh. They make their own herbal oils, vinegars, and blends, and experiment with abandon.

The many fine cooks and food writers whose recipes have appeared in *The Herb Companion* since its debut in 1988 have been on the front edge of this change. They have looked to the rich history of herbal cookery, to the lively and flavorful ethnic cuisines that are transforming the restaurant scene in this country, and to their own gardens for inspiration and guidance in creating unforgettable flavor experiences.

The several hundred recipes in this collection are gleaned from the first five volumes of the magazine. Use them in the same spirit of adventure with which they were created. Increase or decrease the quantities of herbs to suit your or your family's taste. If you don't like tarragon, try thyme. If parsley seems too tame, use basil instead. Be open to new combinations. Taste as you go, and trust your palate. Make these recipes your own.

Linda Ligon
editor, *The Herb Companion*

	BASIL	CORIANDER	DILL	MINT	OREGANO	PARSLEY
Name and Life Cycle	*Ocimum Basilicum;* A	*Coriandrum sativum;* A	*Anethum graveolens;* A	*Mentha spicata, M. x piperita;* HP	*Origanum vulgare;* HP	*Petroselinum crispum;* HB
Flavor	Orange peel and sage	Orange peel and sage	Fresh, aromatic	Sweet, fresh, aromatic	Sharp, aromatic	Refreshing, peppery
Height (ft.)	1 to 2	1 to 2	3	1½	2	1
Exposure	Sun	Sun	Sun	Partial shade	Sun	Sun, partial shade
Soil	Loam rich in humus	Well-drained, rich	Light, well-drained	Moist, rich, well-drained	Well-drained, poor	Heavy, damp
Propagation	Seed	Seed	Seed	Cuttings, division	Seed, cuttings, division	Seed (slow germination)
Part(s) Used	Fresh or dried leaves	Ground seed, fresh leaf (cilantro)	Fresh or dried seeds, stems, leaves	Fresh or dried leaves	Fresh or dried leaves	Frozen or fresh leaves
Meat, Poultry, and Fish	Chopped meat, sausages, lamb, veal, beef, liver, ragouts	Chopped meat, sausage. Leaves: steaks, chops	Lamb steaks and chops, broiled steak, corned beef, creamed chicken, shrimp, fish stock. Leaves: fish	Lamb, ham, veal, ragout, roast beef, roast chicken, fish	Beef, lamb, port, veal, sausages, poultry, fish, calf liver, game, marinades	Beef, lamb, port, veal, poultry, fish, shellfish, marinades
Soups and Stews	Tomato and bean soups, meat stews	Most soups; beef stews, casseroles	Bean, borscht, split pea, and tomato soup; lamb stew	Pea and lentil soup	Vegetable juice cocktail; lentil, onion, bean, beef, game, or tomato soup, meat stews	In soup bouquets, chopped in soups and stews, garnish
Eggs and Cheese	Rarebits, omelets, scrambled and creamed eggs, soufflés	Mexican or spicy egg dishes	Cheese spreads, shirred and scrambled eggs	Cream cheese, cottage cheese, omelets	Cheese spreads, omelets, scrambled or boiled eggs	Deviled or scrambled eggs or omelets
Vegetables and Salads	Tomatoes, eggplant, onion, rutabaga, squash; potato, green, seafood, cucumber salads	Pickled beets; beet and fruit salads	Seafood salads, cocktails, sour cream dressing, cabbage. Seeds: beets, carrots, cauliflower, peas, snap beans, potato salad. Leaves: turnips, pickles	Peas, cabbage, carrots, celery, potatoes, snap beans, spinach; fruit, jellied, green salads; french dressing	Broccoli, beans, tomatoes, carrots, lima beans, peas, mushrooms, onions, potatoes, squash, eggplant; potato, shrimp salad	Most vegetables and salads; creamed vegetables, boiled potatoes, sliced tomatoes
Breads and Desserts	Corn bread and muffins, stuffing (especially duck); fruit compotes	Seed: Poultry stuffing, cookies, gingerbread, baked apples, stewed fruit	Seeds: rye bread, apple dumplings, stewed pears, cake	Fruit compote, custard, ice cream, applesauce, stewed pears, currant jelly	Pizzas, rolls, stuffings	Biscuits, herb breads, muffins, stuffings
Sauces and Gravies	Marinades, butter sauce for fish	Meat sauces	Seeds: fish sauces, beef and other gravies	Mint sauce for lamb	Cream, fish, and spaghetti sauce, other tomato sauces	Cheese sauces, parsley butter
Other Modern Uses	Vinegar, potpourri	Seeds: curry powder, comfits, demitasse. Leaves: Chinese and Mexican cooking	Drawn butter, vinegar	Oil in confectionery; flower vinegar and liqueurs, iced drinks, cranberry juice	Much used in Mexican and Italian cooking	Gratuitous garnishing
Folk and Historic Uses	Repels witches. Tea for colds, menstrual and internal pains.	Seeds good for stomach. Narcotic in large amounts.	Hiccups, swelling, pains, brain. Seed: flatulence, digestion; promotes rest.	Repels moths and mice. Tea helps appetite and digestion, headache, gums, sleeplessness, stomach ache.	Tea for sighing and wambling of stomach, deafness, toothache, bruises. Appetite restorative.	Good for dogs, stomach, dropsy, heart. Stimulates digestive glands.

D o z e n   F a v o r i t e   H e r b s

ROSEMARY	SAGE	SAVORY	SWEET MARJORAM	TARRAGON	THYME
Rosmarinus officinalis; TP	*Salvia officinalis;* HP	*Satureja hortensis;* A *S. montana;* HP	*Origanum majorana;* TP	*Artemisia dracunculus* var. *sativa;* HP	*Thymus vulgaris;* HP
Pungent, resinous	Aromatically bitter, strong, musky	Peppery, spicy, pungent	Fragrant, sweet, slightly resinous	Aniselike	Strong, pungent
5	2	1½ to 2	1	1½	1
Sun	Sun	Sun	Sun	Sun	Sun
Well-drained, lime	Light, well-drained	Average to thin, dry	Dry, well-drained, neutral	Sandy, well-drained	Any
Seed, cuttings	Seed, cuttings, division	Seed. Winter; also cuttings	Seed	Root division every 2 years	Seed, cuttings, or division
Fresh or dried leaves	Fresh or dried leaves	Fresh or dried leaves	Fresh or dried leaves	Fresh, dried, or frozen leaves	Fresh or dried leaves
Beef, game, lamb, port, veal, poultry, salmon, creamed seafood, marinades	Veal and chicken dishes, port pâté, game, beef, sausage, rabbit, lamb, mutton, fish stock	Boiled meats, pâté, lamb, veal, chicken, fish, and seafood, barbecue	Pàtés, sausages, beef, port, veal, pot roasts, fish (especially broiled)	Chicken dishes, seafood, lamb, veal, sweetbreads, turkey, chicken livers, pheasant, tongue	Chopped meat and meat loaf, beef, lamb, mutton, veal, port, fish, shellfish, game
Chicken, pea, and spinach soup	Chowders, consommé, bland cream soups, pork and chicken stews	Potato, bean, pea, and lentil soup; consommés, vegetable juice, chowders; meat stews	Savory stews; pea, tomato, onion, and potato soup; clam chowder	Chicken and tomato soups, chowders, consommés, vegetable juice	Onion, tomato, pea, and vegetable soup, chowders and oyster stew, gumbo; herb bouquet
Deviled or scrambled eggs, omelets	Cottage and cream cheese, cheese omelets and spreads	Scrambled eggs, cream cheese	Omelets, soufflés, scrambled eggs	Cheese spreads, omelets, scrambled eggs	Stuffed and shirred eggs, omelets, cream and cottage cheese
Lentils, mushrooms, peas, potatoes, spinach, squash; fruit salad	Stewed tomatoes, string beans, lima beans, eggplant, brussels sprouts, carrots, onions, and peas; french dressing	Kasha, cabbage, brussels sprouts, turnips, beets; cooking water for asparagus and artichokes; rice, peas, string beans; salads	Avocados, corn, dry beans, mushrooms, eggplant, carrots, lima beans, peas, spinach, green beans; green salad	Broccoli, cauliflower, peas, cabbage, tomatoes, spinach, beans, asparagus, beets; mixed, green, and jellied salads	Asparagus, beans, beets, carrots, onions, peas, potatoes, rice, tomatoes; aspics
Herb bread and stuffing, especially for fish; cookies	Poultry and fish stuffing, chopped in porridge, cheese bread	Meat or poultry stuffing, herb bread; stewed pears and quinces	Poultry stuffing, biscuits, bread	Herb breads, nut wafers	Poultry and vegetable stuffing; biscuits, breads, waffles; lemon thyme in jellies
Cheese, cream, or game sauce	Butter sauce for fish, gravies, brown sauce	Most gravies, sauces	Fish or spaghetti sauce, gravies	Ravigote, cream, bearnaise, and tartar sauces	Meat and seafood sauces
Tea, potpourris	Tea with Middle Eastern foods	Vinegar	Beer flavoring, perfume, strewing herb	Vinegar	Antiseptic; cough medicine and perfume ingredient, bee plant
Strengthens brain and memory, eyesight; for jaundice, wounds, cough, complexion, good luck. Breaks magic spells.	Digestive with pork; snuff. Tea for stomach, head, brain, senses, memory, palsy, sinews.	Relieves colic, beestings, sciatica, clears dull sight, cures lethargy, palsy, and deafness.	Snuff to purge the brain. Good for cold, diseases of the head, stomach, and sinews.	Sweetens breath; dulls taste of medicine. Heals bite of wild beasts, mad dogs, and dragons. Soporific.	Repels moths. Tea: nightmares, nervous headaches, and hangovers. Strengthening bath.

*L*et's
start with
herbs

CHEDDAR, SAGE, AND WALNUT TORTA

This smooth, rich torta makes an elegant appetizer. Choose a high-quality sharp cheddar; its subtle bite invigorates the appetite. The walnuts provide a sweet, crunchy contrast.

1/2 pound cream cheese, softened
3 tablespoons fresh sage leaves, chopped (plus a few whole leaves for garnish)
1/2 pound sharp cheddar cheese such as Cabot Vermont, shredded
1 cup walnuts, chopped (reserve a few walnut halves for garnish)

Place the cream cheese in a food processor with the chopped sage leaves. Blend. Line a 2-cup mold with a double thickness of cheesecloth. Arrange the whole sage leaves in a decorative pattern on the bottom of the mold. Add half the cream cheese mixture, then add shredded cheddar, smoothing out the layer and pressing it slightly. Add the walnuts, again pressing gently. Smooth the remaining cream cheese mixture over the walnuts. Fold the ends of the cheesecloth over the top of the torta mixture and press lightly. Refrigerate the mold overnight.

To unmold, fold back the top of the cheesecloth. Invert a serving plate on top of the mold and flip them over together. Lift off the mold and carefully remove the cheesecloth. Garnish the torta with walnut halves.

BRIE WHEEL

Brie has a wonderful affinity for any number of herbs. A large wheel topped with a variety of herbs and served with bread or crackers is a buffet in itself.

1 wheel of ripe brie (about 5 pounds)
1 cup chopped walnuts
1 cup chopped fresh dill
1/2 cup poppy seeds
1 cup chopped watercress
1 cup slivered almonds
1 cup chopped chives

Cut off the top rind of the brie. Lightly mark the top of the cheese into four pie-shaped wedges with a knife, then divide each wedge into three more wedges, again marking lightly. Sprinkle half the walnuts onto one of the wedge-shaped areas and press them gently into the surface. Repeat the process with half of each of the remaining ingredients, proceeding in order around the wheel. Allow the brie to

Cheddar, Sage, and Walnut Torta, recipe opposite, and Italian Pesto Cheese Torta, recipe on page 6.

stand at room temperature for 30 minutes before serving. The wheel can be loosely wrapped and re-frigerated for as long as 4 hours.

HERB STUFFED OYSTERS

Fresh oysters are a special treat. A savory spinach-tar-ragon stuffing sets off their succulent richness.

1 dozen fresh oysters in the shell
1 10-ounce package frozen chopped spinach, thawed
1/2 stick unsalted butter
2 tablespoons finely minced onion (1/2 small)
2 tablespoons chopped fresh tarragon
1/4 cup chopped fresh Italian or curly parsley
2 tablespoons fresh lemon juice
Hot red pepper sauce to taste
Salt, and freshly ground black pepper
1/4 cup freshly grated parmesan cheese

Preheat the oven to 450° F. Place bottom shell of oys-ters in a single layer in a 9" × 13" baking dish. Place one oyster in each shell. Squeeze all of the moisture out of the spinach.

Melt butter in a medium skillet over medium-high heat. Add onion and sauté until soft, about 5 min-utes. Add spinach, parsley, and tarragon, and cook, stirring, 2 to 3 minutes. Top each oyster with a gen-erous tablespoon of the spinach mixture, and sprin-kle each with 1/2 teaspoon of cheese.

Bake in preheated oven until cheese is golden brown, about 10 minutes.

ITALIAN PESTO CHEESE TORTA

Pine nuts and pesto are layered in between creamy fresh cheeses in this classic Italian torta.

1 pound cream cheese, softened
15 ounces ricotta, drained
1/2 pound fresh mozzarella, drained
10–12 fresh basil leaves
1 cup toasted pine nuts
3/4 cup Pesto (recipe on page 18)
1 teaspoon salt

Line a standard bread pan with a double thickness of fine-weave cheesecloth. Allow enough cheesecloth to fold over the top of the mold after the cheese has been layered. Arrange fresh basil leaves in a deco-rative pattern on the cheesecloth and sprinkle on 1 to 2 tablespoons of the pine nuts.

Combine cream cheese, ricotta, mozzarella, and salt in a food processor (or use an electric mixer) and blend until smooth. Place one-third of the cheese mixture in the pan and smooth it into an even layer. Spread half the pesto over the top and sprinkle on half the remaining pine nuts. Repeat these layers, ending with a cheese layer. Fold the cheesecloth over the top of the cheese and press slightly to even up the mold. Refrigerate 1 to 3 days.

To unmold, press down on the cheesecloth to make sure that the cheese is firmly in place. Fold back the top of the cheesecloth and pull up on the sides a little to loosen the mold. Invert a serving plate over the pan, keeping the cheesecloth away from the top of the mold. Turn over the mold together with the plate, then lift the pan off the cheese. Peel the cheesecloth carefully off the torta.

Variation: Substitute sun-dried tomato pesto for traditional pesto. Arrange whole sun-dried tomatoes, sliced black olives, basil, and pine nuts in a decora-tive pattern in the pan for the top of the torta.

GOAT CHEESE AND PEPPER TORTA

Although this torta is from Provence, its superb taste suggests a Moroccan influence. Choose a mild to ma-ture chèvre, depending on your taste. If goat cheese isn't to your liking, you can substitute feta or a mild blue cheese. The crisp texture of the green and red peppers contrasts delightfully with the smooth spiced cheese.

1 medium onion, finely chopped
2 tablespoons butter
11 ounces goat cheese
4 tablespoons fresh chives, finely chopped
4 tablespoons fresh cilantro, chopped
2 teaspoons cumin seed
1 teaspoon sweet paprika
2 garlic cloves, minced
Dash cayenne pepper
Salt and freshly ground pepper to taste
1 green pepper, chopped
1 red pepper, chopped (plus top for garnish)
Lettuce leaves for garnish
Fresh cilantro sprigs for garnish

Sauté the onion in butter until soft. Place all ingre-dients except peppers and garnishes in a food proces-sor or mixing bowl and blend thoroughly. Line a 3- to 4-cup mold with a double thickness of cheesecloth. Place the red pepper top upside down in the bottom of the mold and sprinkle chopped red and green pepper bits around it. Cover with half the cheese mixture and level the mixture with a spoon. Sprinkle on the remaining pepper bits and add the remaining layer of cheese. Fold the cheesecloth over the top and press it slightly to firm in place. Let the mold set overnight in the refrigerator.

To unmold, fold back the top of the cheesecloth. Invert a serving plate on top of the mold and flip them over together. Lift off the mold and carefully remove the cheesecloth. Garnish the torta with lettuce leaves and fresh cilantro.

HERBED RED PEPPER AND RICOTTA ENVELOPES

Makes 24 to 30 envelopes

*1 large red bell pepper, roasted, peeled, seeded, and cut
    into large pieces*
15 ounces ricotta cheese
1/4 cup fresh basil leaves
1/4 cup fresh parsley leaves
2 cloves garlic
1 teaspoon extra-virgin olive oil
Salt and freshly ground pepper to taste
1/4 cup freshly grated parmesan cheese
2 tablespoons lightly toasted pine nuts (optional)
1 package phyllo dough (20 large sheets)
About 6 tablespoons unsalted butter, melted

Put the red bell pepper into a food processor or blender with about 1/2 cup of ricotta, basil, parsley, garlic, olive oil, and salt and pepper. Puree until smooth. Stir in the parmesan and the rest of the ricotta and blend well. (If all the ricotta is added at the beginning, the filling tends to be runny.) You should now have a generous 2 cups of filling.

To prepare the envelopes, spread two sheets of phyllo on a work surface and brush lightly with butter. With a sharp knife or pizza cutter, cut the phyllo in half lengthwise, then cut each half into equal thirds so there are six equal pieces. Place about 1½ tablespoons of filling on one corner of each piece. Sprinkle a few pine nuts over the filling, if desired. Fold the corner over the filling, fold each side over, and roll up like an envelope, sealing the point with a bit of butter. Cut another double sheet of lightly buttered phyllo into six equal pieces and fold the little packets into envelopes once again. (If the envelopes are not double-wrapped in phyllo, filling will run out while baking.)

Repeat with the rest of the filling and phyllo. Brush the tops of the finished envelopes lightly with butter. At this point, you can place the envelopes on baking sheets, wrap them tightly with plastic wrap, and freeze them for as long as one week before baking. Or place the envelopes on lightly greased baking sheets and bake in a preheated 350° F oven for 10 to 12 minutes or until golden brown.

If the envelopes are frozen, remove them from the freezer about 30 minutes before baking. Preheat oven and place the envelopes on lightly greased baking sheets. They will take a bit longer to bake; about 15 to 18 minutes or until golden brown. Serve hot.

SAVORY PHYLLO TRIANGLES

Serves 6 to 8

We've heard that a Greek cook's definition of happiness is when the amount of filling and the phyllo come out the same. You might need an extra sheet or two of phyllo, depending on how large your teaspoons are.

1/2 pound phyllo dough, about 18 sheets
3 tablespoons unsalted butter, melted
3 tablespoons olive oil
3½ ounces fresh goat cheese, or feta, at room temperature
8 ounces ricotta cheese
*1 bunch scallions, sliced thin and including about 4
    inches of green*
*About 1 tablespoon minced summer savory (12 sprigs),
    or about 3/4 tablespoon minced winter savory
    (8 sprigs)*
Salt and freshly ground black pepper

Thaw the phyllo and keep it covered according to package directions. Warm the melted butter with the olive oil. Thoroughly mix the goat cheese, ricotta, sliced scallions, and minced savory. (Feta may need to be grated or crumbled before mixing with ricotta.) Season the mixture to taste with salt and pepper.

Cut the phyllo into thirds along the length of the dough, and work with one phyllo strip at a time on a baking sheet lightly brushed with the butter-oil mixture. Butter a 2-inch wide section at the end of the strip, and fold the buttered section onto the strip. Then brush the entire strip lightly with the butter-oil mixture. Place a heaping teaspoon of filling on the folded section, then fold the phyllo over it to form a triangle. Brush lightly with butter-oil mixture and fold again to form another triangle. Repeat until the triangle is complete. Brush the top and bottom lightly with butter-oil mixture and place on baking sheet. Repeat until all the triangles have been formed. The recipe may be prepared ahead to this point.

Cover the finished triangles tightly with plastic wrap and store in the refrigerator for up to a day. To serve, preheat the oven to 350° F. Bake the triangles until light golden brown, about 15 to 20 minutes, changing the position of the baking sheets halfway through the baking. Serve hot on a warm platter.

TARRAGON CHICKEN TRIANGLES

Makes 56

Using ready-made phyllo pastry, these elegant appetizers are easier to construct than they look, and freeze beautifully. Make a double batch, and you'll be prepared for any occasion.

1/2 cup chopped walnuts
3 cups water
1 pound boneless, skinless chicken breasts, trimmed of all fat
1/2 cup sour cream
2 tablespoons fresh tarragon, or 2 teaspoons dried
2 tablespoons chopped shallot
1 tablespoon chopped fresh Italian or curly parsley
1 tablespoon chopped chives
1 tablespoon Dijon-style mustard
3/4 teaspoon salt
Pinch freshly ground black pepper
1 pound whole wheat or white phyllo pastry, thawed (you need 21 sheets)
3 sticks unsalted butter, melted

Preheat oven to 350° F. Place walnuts in a single layer on a baking sheet and toast in the preheated oven until nuts smell toasted, 10 to 15 minutes. Cool to room temperature.

Bring the water to a boil in a medium skillet. Add chicken and reduce heat to barely a simmer. Poach the chicken until cooked through, 10 to 15 minutes. Remove chicken to a plate and cool to room temperature. Chop chicken and place in a mixing bowl.

Stir walnuts, sour cream, herbs, shallot, mustard, salt, and pepper into chicken. Taste for seasoning.

Place one sheet of phyllo on a work surface and brush generously with melted butter. Repeat with two more sheets, buttering each. Cut the pastry into 8 long strips. Place a generous teaspoon of filling at the top of each strip. Fold the pastry corner across the filling, and continue folding like a flag to form a triangle. Do not fold too tightly, as filling will expand as it bakes. Place triangles on a baking sheet. Repeat with remaining pastry and filling.

Bake phyllo triangles in a preheated 400° F oven until golden brown, 15 to 20 minutes. Drain on paper towels and let cool about 5 minutes before serving. (Filling gets very hot—it can burn your mouth!)

RICOTTA AND PARSLEY PUFFS

Serves 4 with soup

These pastries make a lovely, savory accompaniment to soup, or can be served before the meal with an aperitif.

8 ounces puff pastry (fresh or frozen)
1 cup ricotta cheese
1 cup minced parsley
1 clove garlic, minced
3 tablespoons grated parmesan cheese
Black pepper

Combine all the ingredients for the filling. Roll out the pastry 1/8 inch thick and cut into 3-inch circles. Place a teaspoon of the filling on half of the circle and moisten the edges with a pastry brush dipped in water. Fold over the other half of the pastry to form a semicircle. Press the edges to seal. Brush with an egg wash, if desired. Bake in a preheated oven at 425° F for 15–20 minutes, or until golden.

BASIL PARMESAN CHEESE STRAWS

Makes 40

Light, flaky, melt-in-your-mouth pastries pack an herbal flavor punch. Frozen puff pastry makes them quick and easy.

1 pound frozen all-butter puff pastry, thawed
2/3 cup grated imported parmesan cheese
2 tablespoons chopped fresh basil, or
*   2 teaspoons dried*
1 large egg yolk
2 teaspoons water

Preheat oven to 350° F. Line two baking sheets with parchment or waxed paper; set aside.

Place one sheet of puff pastry on a lightly floured surface. Sprinkle pastry with 2 tablespoons of the cheese. Press cheese into dough with your fingers. Cover the sheet of pastry with the remaining sheet, sandwiching the cheese in between. Roll the pastry into an 18-by-20-inch rectangle. Sprinkle the pastry with half the remaining cheese and the basil. Press cheese and herbs into the pastry with your fingers.

Bourbon Rosemary Almonds, recipe on page 11, and Tarragon Chicken Triangles, recipe opposite.

Fold pastry in half crosswise. Reroll the pastry into an 18-by-20-inch rectangle.

Beat egg yolk and water together with a fork until combined. Lightly brush pastry with egg glaze and sprinkle with the remaining cheese.

Cut pastry into 40 strips, 1/2-by-18 inches. Twist each strip several times on the baking sheet. (These strips may be baked close together.)

Bake cheese straws in the preheated oven until golden brown, 12 to 15 minutes.

BORAGE FRITTERS WITH CAPERS

Serves 4 to 6

Blanching the borage briefly is necessary to render the leaves bright green and tame their fuzziness. The fritters are in the nature of French *amuses gueules*, little tidbits to tickle the mouth, as fried foods should.

50 borage leaves, about 2 inches long
3/4 cup all-purpose flour
1/4 teaspoon salt
1/2 cup water
4 tablespoons fruity olive oil
2 tablespoons white wine
2 tablespoons nonpareil (small) capers
1 shallot, minced
1 tablespoon white wine vinegar
Salt and freshly ground pepper
2 large egg whites
Peanut or other vegetable oil for frying

Bring a pan of water to a simmer. Place the borage leaves in a sieve and dip them in the water for 2 seconds. Refresh the leaves under cold water and place them between paper towels to dry.

Mix the flour and salt together in a bowl. Whisk in the water, 2 tablespoons of the olive oil, and the wine to make a smooth batter. Cover the batter with plastic wrap and let it stand for an hour or two at room temperature, or overnight in the refrigerator. Let the batter come to room temperature before using it.

Make the sauce by mixing together 1 tablespoon of the capers, half of the minced shallot, 2 tablespoons of the olive oil, and the vinegar. Season with salt and pepper.

A few minutes before frying the fritters, stir the remaining capers and minced shallot into the batter. Beat the egg whites until stiff, but not dry.

Heat 1 inch of vegetable oil to about 360° F. (When the oil is properly heated, a bread cube will be golden brown in 1 minute.)

Fold the beaten egg whites into the batter and place the batter in a shallow baking dish. Place about one-third of the borage leaves on the batter. Using kitchen tongs or a fork, coat the leaves with the batter.

Drop the coated leaves individually into the hot oil. Cook the fritters, turning them once, until they are golden brown, about 1½ minutes. Remove from the oil and drain on paper towels. Keep warm in a 150° F oven. Continue coating and frying the leaves until they have all been cooked. Serve the fritters hot, with the dipping sauce on the side.

SAVORY CHEDDAR SPREAD WITH SHERRY

Makes about 2 cups

This spread uses a dry sherry, which gives it a bit of a tang at first, but it mellows quickly. (If you don't like sherry, use 1/4 cup beer instead.) It is best made at least a day in advance. It will keep refrigerated for a week to 10 days and tastes best if allowed to stand at room temperature for 15 to 20 minutes before serving.

1/2 pound sharp cheddar cheese, grated
8 tablespoons unsalted butter, at cool room temperature
3 tablespoons dry sherry
1 teaspoon Dijon-style mustard
3 dashes Angostura bitters
2 small pinches cayenne pepper
1 teaspoon dried winter savory, crumbled, or
*   1 tablespoon fresh winter savory leaves*
3 tablespoons freshly chopped Italian parsley

Combine the cheese and butter in a food processor and process until blended. Add the sherry, mustard, bitters, cayenne, and savory and process until smooth. Add the chopped parsley and process until just blended. Pack into a 2-cup crock and refrigerate.

BOURSIN WITH FINO VERDE BASIL

Makes 1 cup

Fine green basil is perfectly suited for this recipe; the tiny leaves are packed with flavor but are time-consuming to harvest, so reserve it for those recipes where a little bit goes a long way.

2 cloves garlic, peeled
1/2 cup fresh 'Fino Verde' basil leaves
1/4 cup chives
1/4 cup parsley leaves

8 ounces cream cheese
1/4 cup black olives, pitted

In a food processor, combine the garlic and herbs. Blend in the cream cheese until smooth. Add the olives and coarsely chop. Transfer to a small bowl and garnish with a sprig of fresh basil in the center. Make ahead and refrigerate so that the flavors can meld. Serve with crackers or generously spread on pieces of French bread topped with thin slices of roast beef.

BOURBON ROSEMARY ALMONDS

Makes 3 cups

Pungent rosemary and cumin, mellowed with brown sugar and bourbon, blend and linger in these crunchy, nutty treats . . . just one more!

3 cups blanched whole almonds
1 cup (packed) light brown sugar
1/4 cup bourbon
2 tablespoons water
2 tablespoons dried rosemary, crumbled, or
    1/3 cup chopped fresh rosemary
2 teaspoons ground cumin
1 teaspoon coarse salt
1/4 teaspoon cayenne

Preheat oven to 375° F. Place almonds in a single layer on a baking sheet and toast in the preheated oven until golden brown and fragrant, 15 to 20 minutes. Remove from the oven and set aside.

Heat brown sugar, bourbon, and water to a boil in a small saucepan over medium heat. Continue boiling for 10 minutes. Combine remaining ingredients together in a small bowl. When syrup is finished, add almonds and stir to coat completely. Stir in seasonings, mixing well.

Transfer nuts to a buttered baking sheet and separate with a fork while still warm. Cool before serving, and store in a can with a tight-fitting lid.

SEEDED SAGE AND CHEDDAR WAFERS

Makes 6 dozen

2 tablespoons sesame seeds
2 tablespoons poppy seeds
3 tablespoons chopped fresh sage, or 1 tablespoon dried
1½ cups unbleached all-purpose flour
1/2 teaspoon cayenne

1/2 pound sharp white cheddar cheese, cut into 1/2-inch chunks
1 stick unsalted butter, cut into tablespoon pieces

Preheat oven to 400° F.

Toast sesame seeds in a medium skillet over medium-low heat until golden brown, shaking the skillet continuously. Transfer the seeds to a large bowl. Add poppy seeds, sage, flour, and cayenne to bowl and stir to combine.

Chop cheese in food processor with the metal blade until very fine. Add flour mixture and butter and process until the dough forms a ball.

Transfer dough to a lightly floured surface and roll into a 12-inch log. Cut dough into 1/8-inch thick slices and place on a baking sheet. Bake wafers in preheated oven until golden brown around the edges, 10 to 12 minutes.

PARMESAN SAGE LEAVES

2/3 cup cake flour
2 tablespoons grated fresh Parmesan cheese
Pinch cayenne pepper
Pinch salt
2 teaspoons olive oil
1/3 cup beer (not dark)
1 large egg, separated
30 to 36 large sage leaves, gently washed and dried
    with paper towels
Vegetable oil, for frying
Lemon wedges

Whisk flour, cheese, cayenne, salt, olive oil, beer, and egg yolk together until smooth. Cover and let rest 1 to 3 hours in a warm place. Beat egg white until stiff but not dry. Fold into batter with a rubber spatula.

Heat 1 inch of oil in a wok or skillet to 360° F. Dip sage leaves in batter and fry in batches until golden brown. Drain on paper towels. Serve immediately or keep warm in a 200° F oven. Squeeze with lemon juice. Serve as an hors d'oeuvres or as an accompaniment to grilled meats.

HERBED YOGURT CHEESE

Makes 1 cup

Loaded with a tantalizing blend of herbs and spices, this creamy spread is low in calories, cholesterol, and effort. You'll want to make it often, tailoring the seasonings to what's fresh in the garden or handy on the shelf.

2 cups plain low-fat yogurt
2 tablespoons chopped fresh Italian or curly parsley
1 teaspoon minced garlic
1 teaspoon minced shallot
1/2 teaspoon salt
1 teaspoon dried rosemary
1/2 teaspoon whole celery seed
1/2 teaspoon dried thyme
1/4 teaspoon ground coriander
1/4 teaspoon cayenne

Stir all ingredients together in a bowl.

Line a coffee filter holder from a coffee maker with a paper coffee filter. Fill the filter with the yogurt mixture. Place filter holder over a bowl to catch liquid. Cover with foil and place in the refrigerator. Let yogurt drain for 12 to 24 hours. (The longer it drains, the creamier the cheese will be.)

Place cheese in a crock and serve with crackers.

HERB CRACKERS

Makes about 8 dozen 1¹⁄₂ -inch crackers

These crackers are much more substantial than anything store-bought—a bit thicker, buttery, and more flavorful. The rye flour is tasty, but you could substitute whole wheat flour. The crackers will keep for a week to 10 days in a tightly closed tin. You may make the dough a day or two in advance, refrigerate it, then let it come to cool room temperature before rolling it out.

1¹⁄₂ cups unbleached flour
1/2 cup rye flour
1/2 teaspoon salt
1¹⁄₂ teaspoons baking powder
8 tablespoons unsalted butter,
    cut into 8 pieces
1 extra large egg
1 tablespoon horseradish mustard·
1 teaspoon fresh thyme leaves, minced, or scant
    1/2 teaspoon dried thyme leaves, crumbled
3 tablespoons freshly snipped garlic chives
4 tablespoons ice water

Preheat the oven to 400° F.

Combine the dry ingredients in a food processor and pulse to blend. Add the butter and process until butter is in pea-size pieces. Add the egg and mustard and mix until just blended. Add the herbs and process a few seconds more. Add the ice water and pulse until the dough just starts to come together.

Turn the dough onto a lightly floured pastry mar-ble or board and knead for two or three minutes. Divide the dough into two parts; flatten them into disks about 1/4 inch thick. Wrap one in plastic and refrigerate until ready to roll. Roll the first piece of dough about 1/8 inch thick, lightly flouring and turning the dough as necessary.

Cut the dough with a biscuit cutter or cookie cutters. For simple, homey-looking crackers, cut the dough diagonally into 1¹⁄₂-inch strips with a fluted ravioli cutter, then cut lines 1¹⁄₂ inches apart across the strips to make diamonds. You may prick each cracker with a fork a few times, but it is not necessary.

Bake the crackers on ungreased baking sheets for 10 minutes, or until they just begin to turn golden. (While the first batch is baking, roll out the other piece of dough.) Remove crackers to cooling racks. When completely cool, store in tins.

HERBED CREAM CHEESE AND WATERCRESS SANDWICHES

Makes 40 to 50 tea sandwiches

These tea sandwiches are not lily-livered; they're full of flavor. If you're using a baguette rather than a miniature loaf of pumpernickel, the sandwiches are better if assembled and served right away, rather than refrigerated.

1 pound cream cheese, softened
1 tablespoon milk or half-and-half
1 large clove garlic
1/4 cup basil leaves or dill sprigs, loosely packed
1/4 cup parsley and/or watercress leaves, tightly packed
1 tablespoon preserved tarragon leaves or 1¹⁄₂ tablespoons
    fresh tarragon leaves and 1¹⁄₂ teaspoons tarragon
    vinegar
2 dashes Angostura bitters
Pinch cayenne pepper
Salt to taste

Combine the cream cheese, milk, and garlic in a food processor or blender and process until smooth. Add the rest of the ingredients and process, stopping to scrape down the sides, until blended. Refrigerate the herbed cream cheese for at least an hour so the flavors can develop; it will keep for 5 to 7 days in the refrigerator if tightly wrapped. Allow to stand at room temperature for 15 to 20 minutes before spreading.

1 miniature loaf pumpernickel or baguette, thinly sliced
1 bunch watercress, washed and picked over
1 or 2 large cucumbers, peeled and thinly sliced

Have all ingredients ready for assembly. Spread each slice of bread generously with the herbed cream cheese. Place two sprigs of watercress on each sandwich so that the leaves hang over the edges a little. Place a slice of cucumber on top of each sandwich so that the cress sprigs are peeking out from underneath. If the pumpernickel slices are a little larger, you can use two slices of cucumber. The sandwiches can be made a few hours ahead of time, layered with waxed paper in between layers, and kept tightly wrapped in the refrigerator. Allow to come to cool room temperature before serving.

STUFFED MUSHROOMS WITH OREGANO

Serves 6 to 12

This dish capitalizes on the absorbent property of mushrooms; here, they are cooked in a little wine. These popular appetizers lend themselves to several variations: you may cook them in broth rather than wine, use marjoram instead of oregano, or add a few tiny imported canned clams to the stuffing and cook the mushrooms in the clam juice. The recipe is easily doubled.

12 large mushrooms
3 tablespoons olive oil
1 garlic clove, minced
1/3 cup chopped parsley
1 tablespoon chopped fresh oregano or 1 scant teaspoon crumbled dried oregano
1/3 cup fine dry bread crumbs
1/4 cup freshly grated parmesan cheese
Salt and freshly ground pepper
1/2 cup dry white wine

Carefully wipe the mushrooms clean. Remove and mince the stems. Heat the olive oil in a small skillet and sauté the stems with the garlic over moderate heat for about 3 minutes.

Preheat the oven to 350° F.

Remove the mixture from the heat and add the parsley, oregano, bread crumbs, and parmesan cheese. Season well with salt and pepper, and blend the mixture well.

Pack enough stuffing into each mushroom cap to form a mound. Arrange the mushrooms in a lightly buttered 11-by-8-inch gratin dish, pour the wine into the dish, and bake for 10 minutes.

Place the dish under a preheated broiler approximately 2 inches from the heat for about 1 minute, or until the tops of the mushrooms are golden brown. Transfer the mushrooms with a slotted spatula to a warm platter. Serve hot or warm.

FRITTATA WITH PEAS, NEW POTATOES, AND MINT

Makes 24 to 30 pieces

Fresh garden peas make this frittata especially delicious, but frozen peas work just fine. If you are using a mild-tasting mint like spearmint, use the larger amount; if you are using a strong peppermint, use less.

Prepare this dish in a 10- or 12-inch sauté pan or skillet with an ovenproof handle, turn it out to cool, then cut it into 1/2-inch squares or diamonds. It can also be baked in buttered 1³/₄-inch muffin tins at 350° F for 12 to 15 minutes or until set.

5 extra-large eggs at room temperature
1 tablespoon water
1¹/₂ to 2 tablespoons finely minced mint leaves
2 tablespoons finely minced parsley, preferably Italian flat-leaved
1/2 cup freshly grated parmesan cheese
Few grindings nutmeg
Salt and freshly ground pepper to taste
2 tablespoons unsalted butter
1/2 pound new potatoes, cut into 1/2-inch dice and cooked until just tender (about 1¹/₂ cups)
1 cup sweet peas, fresh, or frozen and thawed
1/4 cup finely chopped onion, sautéed for 2 to 3 minutes in 1 tablespoon unsalted butter
Parmesan for garnish
Mint leaves to garnish the platter

In a large bowl, beat the eggs with the water. Add the mint, parsley, parmesan, nutmeg, salt, and pepper, and blend well.

Melt the butter in a large sauté pan over medium heat. Add the potatoes, peas, and onion to the egg mixture and stir well. Pour the egg and vegetable mixture into the hot pan and cook over medium heat for about 5 minutes.

Preheat the broiler. Using a spatula, loosen the edges of the frittata around the pan as it cooks. After about 5 to 7 minutes, when the eggs are beginning to set, gently lift an edge and look under. When the underside appears to be a deep golden brown, remove from heat and place the entire pan under the broiler. Keep a close eye on the frittata under the broiler; it will take only 2 to 3 minutes to turn deep golden brown on top.

Remove the pan from the broiler, loosen the frittata again, and carefully slide it onto a serving platter. Sprinkle it lightly with parmesan. Cool for a few minutes and serve warm, or let cool to room temperature. The frittata can be made a few hours in advance; keep loosely covered at room temperature. It can be gently reheated in a 300° F oven until hot, if desired.

QUESO FLAMEADO (SPICY BROILED CHEESE)

This broiled cheese specialty of northern Mexico may be assembled ahead of time, then broiled at the last minute. A great accompaniment for barbecue. Serve with warm tortillas or tostada chips and bowls of condiments such as chopped cilantro, chopped tomatoes, avocado wedges, chopped green onions, and salsa picante.

1 pound grated cheese (cheddar, monterey jack, muenster, or a combination of several)
2–4 cloves garlic, minced
6 Anaheim or poblano chiles, roasted and peeled and cut in strips 1–2 inch wide by 3 inches long
1–2 jalapeño chiles, chopped (optional)
3 green onions, chopped
1/2 teaspoon dried or 1/2 teaspoons fresh Mexican oregano
1 tomato, chopped
2 tablespoons fresh chopped cilantro

Mix grated cheese, garlic, peppers, half the onions and the oregano in a 9-by-12-inch earthenware *cazuela* which can tolerate broiling. Bake at 450° F until bubbly, stirring occasionally. Add the tomato and broil until golden brown. Sprinkle with remaining onions and the chopped cilantro. Garnish with festive condiments. Epazote may be substituted for cilantro when white cheese is used. Look for Oaxacan-type string cheese available in some specialty markets.

SAGE AND POBLANO CHEESE

Makes about 2 cups

Sage is good with many roasted and peeled green chiles, but it is especially wonderful with poblanos. These are sold fresh in late summer, and are often used for chiles rellenos. If you cannot find poblanos, use fresh New Mexico green chiles with a little bite. Anaheims may be used instead, but they need the addition of a jalapeño to provide some heat. Sage and poblano cheese makes a different and delicious quesadilla or omelet filling. It is also tasty spread on strips of sweet peppers, or on croutons or crackers.

5 ounces fresh goat cheese, crumbled
1/2 pound ricotta cheese
3 large roasted and peeled poblano chiles, cut in small dice (about 1/3 cup diced chiles)
1/2 teaspoon toasted and ground coriander seed
8 to 10 large sage leaves, finely shredded
Salt to taste

Combine the goat cheese well with the ricotta. Stir in the diced poblanos, the ground coriander, and the shredded sage. Cover the cheese and let it stand for an hour or so. Add salt if necessary.

The cheese may be stored tightly covered in the refrigerator for 5 or 6 days. Serve the cheese at cool room temperature, if you are not using it in cooking.

HERB PIE

Makes 1 eight-inch pie

1 cup cooked, chopped sorrel leaves
1 cup cooked, chopped nettle leaves
1/2 cup cooked, chopped plantain leaves
1/2 cup cooked, chopped lamb's-quarters
1 tablespoon fresh, chopped lovage
1 small bunch chives or scallions, chopped
4 eggs, beaten with 1 cup light cream
1/2 cup chopped mushrooms
1 tablespoon fresh, chopped parsley
1 cup shredded mozzarella cheese
2 tablespoons butter
Salt and pepper
1 eight-inch pie shell, unbaked

Sauté mushrooms and chives in butter. Add to greens in large bowl. Add other ingredients except pie shell, reserving 2 tablespoons of cheese. Spread in pie shell and sprinkle with reserved cheese. Bake at 400° F for 10 minutes, then lower heat to 350° and cook 20 minutes longer, or until filling is set and golden brown.

Queso Flameado (Spicy Broiled Cheese), recipe opposite.

Fresh Herb Pizza

Pizzas come in many varieties. One can find pizza in its native Italy, in the south of France, and in England. Pizza comes with all sorts of exotic (and completely un-Italian) embellishments such as "Thai chicken" or "Peking duck". Yet the best pizzas are the ones we bake on our own pizza stones in our own ovens, topped with tomatoes from our own gardens (or, in winter, from the freezer), a light, judicious sprinkling of our favorite cheeses, and a dense coating of freshly picked green herbs.

Pizza itself is almost as old as civilized society. The ancient Romans ate something described as "bread with a relish" for breakfast, and the remains of "pizza" have been found in Pompeii (minus the tomatoes, though; the tomato didn't appear in Europe until the sixteenth century). Pizza was the fast food of the Mediterranean world, the sandwich of ancient humanity, convenient to handle because of the thick lip around its edge.

Since ancient times, men and women throughout the Mediterranean world have been topping flat breads of one type or another with the bounty of the area in which they lived. Noted food historian Waverley Root says that in Liguria (the region surrounding Genoa), "pizza" traditionally contained no tomatoes but plenty of mussels, mushrooms, ham, black olives, or anchovies. The classic Roman pizza contains no tomatoes but plenty of onions, whereas pizza alla napoletana is filled with buffalo-milk mozzarella, tomato, basil or oregano, and anchovies. In the south of France, pissaladière is rectangular and topped with onions, black olives, and anchovy fillets.

The possibilities for interesting pizza toppings today are limitless. They range from good olive oil, freshly picked herbs, and a sprinkling of parmesan cheese to more elaborate sauces and an array of fresh herbs and cheeses. Pizza is simple to make and a delight to serve and eat, and we encourage you to experiment with whatever comes out of the garden—or the freshest grocery-store fare available—to see what kind of "bread with a relish" you can create.

TIPS FOR BETTER PIZZA

—Pizza dough should be softer and more moist than a regular bread dough. This will make for a light, crispy crust.

—Unbaked pizza dough can be frozen in a freezer-weight plastic bag with the air squeezed out of it. Allow room for the dough to rise in the bag when it comes out of the freezer.

—You can add herbs to the dough; the amount will depend upon the effect you want to achieve and the herb in question. It takes only a little rosemary or sage to flavor a dough, whereas you need a lot of chives, parsley, or summer savory if the herb is to be noticed. We prefer to save the herbs for the top of the pizza, where they will get more well-deserved attention.

—Pizza must be cooked in a very hot oven, 500° F or hotter. Preheat it for at least 1/2 hour and don't open the oven door for any longer than is absolutely necessary.

—Pizza can be cooked on either a cookie sheet or a pizza pan, but for an exceptional crust, use a pizza or baking stone. This causes both the bottom and the top of the pizza to cook at the same time and gives a nice, even brown and an "oven rise" to the crust. Preheat the stone as you preheat the oven. If you use a stone, you'll also need a pizza peel, or paddle (available at gourmet shops), to form the pizza on and to transfer it to and from the hot stone in the oven.

—Pizza dough can be mixed and used right away without a rising period. However, letting the dough rise for an hour or so helps to develop a more complex texture and flavor.

—Minimize the liquid in your chosen topping. Italian plum tomatoes (such as Roma) contain proportionally less juice than others and are therefore the tomato of choice for sauces and pizza.

—Go light on the heavy ingredients such as tomatoes, cheeses, and sausage, but use a heavier hand when adding the lighter ones—fresh herbs, garlic, and vegetables.

—If you put herbs on the pizza before you bake it, they will be quite dry by the time the pizza comes out of the oven. Some people like it that way, but we prefer the fresh-from-the-garden flavor of freshly chopped herbs sprinkled over the pizza *after* it comes out of the oven. Some herbs, such as cilantro, can be added *only* after the pizza is out of the oven; at high temperatures, their aromatic oils volatilize very quickly, and you'll be left with nothing but tasteless green specks.

BASIC PIZZA DOUGH

Makes 2 medium pizzas

The amount of water needed to moisten the dough will vary with the humidity and with the type of flour you use. We recommend using up to one cup of freshly milled whole wheat flour.

1 to 1¼ cups warm water
1 package yeast
1 teaspoon sugar
3 to 4 cups flour
2 tablespoons olive oil
1 teaspoon salt

Soften the yeast in warm water with the sugar until it starts to foam. Meanwhile, combine the flour, olive oil, and salt in a large bowl. Add the yeast mixture and mix, first with a spoon and then with hands, until the dough pulls away from the sides of the bowl. At this point, you may freeze it for later use or allow it to rise for an hour (optional) and punch down.

Roll dough out to desired thickness and shape, and place in pizza pan or on a pizza peel sprinkled with flour or corn meal. Add topping and bake in preheated 500° F oven for 10 to 12 minutes.

PIZZA NIÇOISE

This pizza contains the flavors of the south of France—olives, tomatoes, garlic, onions, and fresh herbs.

1/2 cup "Plain Tomato" Pizza Sauce (below)
3 ounces smoked provolone or gouda cheese
Cheddar cheese to taste
1 small yellow onion, thinly sliced
1 small green pepper, thinly sliced
20 black olives, pitted (preferably niçoise or nyons)
2 to 3 cloves garlic, finely minced
Bunch of freshly chopped herbes de Provence
Freshly grated parmesan cheese

Roll the dough and sauce it lightly. Add the smoked cheese and cheddar, then the onion, pepper, and olives. Sprinkle on the minced garlic, chopped fresh herbs, and parmesan cheese, and bake at 500° F for about 12 minutes.

TWO-CHEESE-AND-THREE-BASIL PIZZA

If you don't have easy access to anise or cinnamon basil, don't despair; this pizza is delicious with plain ol' sweet basil. Sharp cheddar and mozzarella cheese may be added.

1 tablespoon olive oil
1 or 2 cloves garlic, minced
1 tomato, thinly sliced
2 ounces goat cheese
2 to 3 tablespoons parmesan cheese
Fresh anise basil leaves
Fresh cinnamon basil leaves
Fresh sweet basil leaves

Roll the dough and brush very lightly with the olive oil. Arrange slices of tomato around the pizza, then sprinkle with dots of goat cheese and parmesan and the minced garlic. Bake for about 10 minutes at 500° F. When the pizza comes out of the oven, roll the basil leaves into a cylinder, slice thinly, and sprinkle over the top.

"PLAIN TOMATO" PIZZA SAUCE

Makes enough for 4 pizzas

This sauce freezes very well.

4 pounds Italian plum tomatoes
2 tablespoons olive oil
1 small red onion
4 to 5 cloves garlic
Chopped fresh parsley
Salt and pepper to taste
Dash red pepper flakes

Blanch tomatoes for 10 to 30 seconds in a big pot of boiling water. Cool briefly in cold water, then cut off stem ends and slip off skins. Chop by hand or puree in batches in a blender.

Sauté onion and garlic in olive oil in a large non-corrodible pan. When onions are translucent, add tomato and parsley and simmer, uncovered, for 5 to 10 minutes longer. Add salt, pepper, and red pepper to taste.

*S*avory
sauces &
stuffings

A BASIC BASIL PESTO

Makes about 1¹/₂ cups

2 packed cups fresh basil leaves, washed and dried
2 cloves garlic
1/2 cup pine nuts
1/2 cup freshly grated parmesan cheese
3/4 cup olive oil
Freshly grated black pepper, to taste

Chop basil and garlic to a coarse paste in blender or food processor. Add nuts and cheese, and process briefly. Add olive oil in a thin, steady stream while continuing to process.

Variations: Substitute pecans for the pine nuts. Or use lemon basil with almonds; cilantro with toasted pumpkin seeds; oregano with walnuts; or mint with cashews.

PURPLE BASIL PESTO

Makes 1 cup

This pesto variation makes a great sauce with sautéed strips of sweet Italian peppers and linguini.

2 cups 'Opal' or 'Purple Ruffles' basil leaves
2 tablespoons sun-dried tomatoes
2 cloves garlic
6 tablespoons asiago or parmesan cheese
1/3 cup toasted pine nuts or walnuts
1/2 cup olive oil

Combine all ingredients except oil in blender or food processor. Slowly add oil. Blend to desired consistency and toss on freshly cooked pasta.

CHEESE-POTTED BASIL

A handy jar of succulent cheese-potted basil tucked in the refrigerator will find a multitude of uses. It will keep for months, if you can resist using it all right away. Add it to pestos, sprinkle it on pasta, spread it on crusty french bread, use your imagination.

2 cups freshly grated parmesan cheese
2 cups fresh basil
2 cloves garlic
1/2 cup pine nuts, pecans, or walnuts
Olive oil

Chop basil, garlic, and nuts together in a blender or food processor to make a coarse paste. Layer this mixture in a pint jar with the cheese, starting and

Purple Basil Pesto, recipe opposite, tops linguine and sweet Italian peppers.

ending with a cheese layer. Pack the layers tightly. Top with 1/2 inch of olive oil. Cover tightly and refrigerate.

FIERY JALAPEÑO PESTO

Makes about 2 cups

Use this pesto for seasoning vegetables, meats, sauces, or pasta, or as a base for salad dressing or marinade. You can using small amounts directly from the freezer.

1 cup fresh jalapeño peppers, stems removed
2 large cloves garlic, each peeled and cut in 4 pieces
1 cup firmly packed fresh basil leaves
1 cup firmly packed fresh cilantro leaves
1 teaspoon freshly ground cumin seed
1/2 to 2/3 cup extra virgin olive oil
1/2 cup freshly grated parmesan cheese
1/2 cup walnuts or pine nuts
1/2 teaspoon salt, if needed, depending on saltiness of cheese
1 tablespoon white wine vinegar

Combine jalapeños, herbs, ground cumin seed, and olive oil in food processor or blender container. Process until smooth. Add remaining ingredients, pulsing several times to mix completely. Taste for seasoning; adjust salt and vinegar as needed. Refrigerate up to 2 weeks; freeze for long-term storage. Reblend if liquids appear when thawed after freezing.

SORREL CHIFFONADE

Serve this tart, creamy, bright green sauce over grilled fish or chicken, or with tiny, boiled new potatoes.

3 tablespoons unsalted butter
1 shallot, finely chopped
3 cups finely shredded sorrel

Melt the butter in a heavy skillet over medium heat, and wilt the shallot in butter until it is limp. Add shredded sorrel and cook, stirring and mashing with a wooden spoon, until the mixture forms a smooth mass. Will keep, refrigerated, for several weeks.

CREAMY TARRAGON SAUCE

Makes 3/4 cup

This all-purpose recipe can be used as a dip with crackers and vegetables, as salad dressing, or as a sauce over cooked chicken, fish, or eggs.

1/2 teaspoon fresh tarragon
1 tablespoon Dijon-style mustard
1 tablespoon mayonnaise
1 tablespoon olive oil
1 tablespoon white wine vinegar
1/2 cup yogurt

Whisk together tarragon, mustard, mayonnaise, olive oil, and vinegar until creamy. Stir in yogurt. Allow flavors to meld for 1 hour before using.

MARY PARROT'S SECRET ROSE GERANIUM SYRUP

Buy a two-quart jar of good-quality corn syrup. Soak off the label. Pour out and reserve 3/4 cup of the syrup.

Gather fresh rose geranium leaves on a sunny day. Dr. Livingston, Cinnamon Rose, or the old fashioned Rose yield the best flavor. Do not wash. Remove petioles and force leaves into the jar of syrup. Cap. Set in a sunny window for three to five days. Taste syrup. If not enough rose flavor has been absorbed, set in the sun another three to five days. Remove leaves. Add a few drops of beet juice from canned or fresh-cooked beets for coloring to the reserved syrup. Stir well. Pour into the larger jar of syrup and stir well. Cap. Put finished syrup in a sunny window for a week, then store in a dark place.

Although slightly different in sweetness from traditional sugar syrup, this is quite thick and a very good syrup to use over vanilla ice cream, puddings, or fruit.

Rose Geranium Syrup captures the essence of summer. Use it during the winter months to sweeten tea, pour it over vanilla ice cream, or use as a marinade for a fresh fruit salad. Also good with custards, whipped cream, and as topping for baked pears.

MINT CHIMICHURRI

Makes 2 cups

This South American classic condiment resembles a very strong vinaigrette. It can be brushed onto meats before grilling or smeared onto vegetables, and is often served in a shaker bottle at the table. If fresh bay leaves aren't available, omit bay altogether.

6 to 8 large cloves garlic, each cut into 4 to 6 pieces
2 cups hard-packed parsley leaves and tender stems (preferably flat-leaved)
1/2 cup hard-packed spearmint or red-stem apple mint leaves and tender stems
4 tablespoons Mexican mint marigold leaves and tender stems
4 tablespoons fresh cilantro leaves and tender stems
4 fresh bay leaves, midribs removed
Dash crushed red peppers or ground cayenne
3/4 cup white wine or cider vinegar
3/4 cup extra virgin olive oil
1/2 teaspoon salt

Combine garlic and herbs in processor and finely chop. Add vinegar, olive oil, and salt, and process just to mix; do not overprocess. Refrigerate at least 24 hours to mellow flavors before using.

MINT AND TOMATILLO SALSA

Makes about 2 cups

Somewhat unusual but complementary flavors make this salsa special. Use it as you would any table salsa: for garnishing tacos, grilled meat, poultry, and fish; and with tortilla chips. When vine-ripened tomatoes are in season, you may want to add a small one to the salsa.

1/4 pound fresh tomatillos
2 or 3 serrano or jalapeño chiles, seeded and diced fine
3 or 4 green onions with some green, sliced thin
About 1 teaspoon white vinegar
1 teaspoon olive oil
2 to 2 1/2 tablespoons chopped fresh mint leaves
Salt to taste
Optional: 1 small ripe tomato, cut in fine dice

Leaving their papery husks attached, roast the tomatillos in a dry skillet over medium heat to bring out their flavor. Turn them several times as they cook. In about 10 minutes they will have blackened spots all over, and they will have a sweet aroma. Remove the husks, and cut the tomatillos in fine dice.

Place the vegetables in a bowl. Stir in the vinegar, oil, and mint leaves. Season with salt. Add the tomato if desired.

CHILES EN ESCABECHE WITH OREGANO

Serves 4 to 6

A big platter of colorful, taste-tingling chiles and peppers is a very southwestern way to brighten and lighten a meal of meat and masa. These accompany filling dishes such as adovados (red chile stews), beans, enchiladas, burritos, chorizo, and grilled meats very well. This is a fresh, light escabeche, with less vinegar than usual. The escabeche may be prepared ahead and kept refrigerated for two or three days. Its character then will be different from when it is served fresh, but it is still good. If red hot cherry peppers are not available, add an extra serrano and jalapeño.

1/4 cup white wine vinegar
2 cups water
1 teaspoon salt
1/2 teaspoon sugar
4 medium sweet peppers: red, green, yellow, and purple, if available
3 or 4 jalapeños
2 hot red cherry peppers
1 large sweet onion
2 tablespoons olive oil
2 tablespoons fresh oregano leaves, chopped coarse

Bring the vinegar, water, salt, and sugar to a boil in a noncorrodible saucepan. Make sure that the sugar and salt are dissolved and remove the liquid from the heat.

Stem and seed the sweet peppers and chiles. Cut the sweet peppers into lengthwise strips about 1/4 inch wide. Cut the chiles into lengthwise slivers. Peel the onion and cut it into lengthwise slivers.

Place the vegetables in a glass or stainless bowl and pour the pickling liquid over them. Mix in the olive oil and oregano. Cover the bowl and marinate in the refrigerator for 3 hours before serving. Drain the liquid from the escabeche before serving or storing. Serve at cool room temperature.

HERBAL CHEESE STUFFING

Makes about 2 cups

Use this rich stuffing to enhance boneless chicken breasts, quail, fish, veal or lamb chops, mushrooms, pastry, or pasta.

8 ounces cream cheese
4 ounces ricotta or cottage cheese
1 large clove garlic, minced or mashed
2 eggs, beaten
2 tablespoons finely chopped fresh chives or green onion
2 tablespoons finely chopped fresh parsley
*2 to 3 tablespoons finely chopped fresh (or 2 to 4
    teaspoons dried) herbs or your choice: sweet marjoram,
    tarragon, rosemary, sage, thyme, basil, or bay*
*1/2 to 3/4 cup soft white bread crumbs (firm, homestyle
    bread)*
Salt and pepper to taste

Combine cheeses with eggs and seasonings and mix well. Add bread crumbs and blend with a fork, being careful not to overmix.

MUSHROOM CAVIAR STUFFING

Makes about 2 cups

This is a versatile stuffing that's suitable for whole fish or fillets, chicken breasts, Cornish game hens, pork or veal loin or chops, or whole vegetables. It can also double as an appetizer dip or as a sauce for beef or pork.

*3 tablespoons butter, margarine, or
    olive oil*
4 medium shallots, chopped
2 tablespoons chopped green onions
1 large clove garlic, crushed
1/2 pound mushrooms, cleaned and chopped or sliced
2 tablespoons dry white wine
*1 tablespoon chopped fresh dill, tarragon, Mexican mint
    marigold, or sweet marjoram*
2 tablespoons sour cream
1 raw egg, beaten
2 tablespoons chopped walnuts, pine nuts or pecans
1/2 cup soft white bread crumbs
1 tablespoons chopped fresh parsley
Salt and freshly ground black pepper to taste

Adding a little at a time, sauté shallots, onions, garlic, and mushrooms in butter or oil over high heat, being careful not to burn. Add wine, sour cream, and seasonings, then cook until almost all liquids are evaporated. Remove from heat and cool slightly.

Add beaten egg, nuts, and bread crumbs, mixing gently until well combined. Stir in parsley and season with salt and pepper. Cook a tablespoon of mixture in a small greased skillet to check seasonings, and adjust as needed.

FABULOUS FAJITA OR CHICKEN MARINADE WITH CILANTRO, CITRUS, AND GOLD TEQUILA

Serves 4 to 6

Cilantro's refreshing flavor mingles with citrus and gold tequila in this robust marinade. Serve marinated and grilled meat or chicken with warm tortillas, avocado wedges, grilled onions, and your favorite salsa picante.

4 cloves garlic, minced
3 tablespoons gold tequila
2 tablespoons fresh lime juice
2 tablespoons fresh orange juice
*2 tablespoons oregano-chile-garlic vinegar or
    red wine vinegar*
1½ teaspoons grated orange zest
1/2 teaspoon crushed dried red chiles
1/2 teaspoon freshly ground black pepper
1/2 teaspoon dried Mexican oregano
1/2 teaspoon brown sugar
4 tablespoons olive oil
3 tablespoons freshly chopped cilantro

Mix ingredients together in a bowl. Marinate meat or chicken in mixture 2 to 4 hours or overnight. For a special treat, wrap marinated chicken around an hoja santa leaf and bake in the oven until tender.

RED WINE VINEGAR MARINADE

This is an excellent marinade for grilled chicken.

1/2 cup Dijon-style mustard
1/4 cup red wine vinegar
1/4 cup lemon juice
6 cloves garlic
3 tablespoons (or more) fresh herbes de Provence
1/2 cup olive oil

Combine all ingredients in a blender and whir until smooth.

Herbal Cheese Stuffing, recipe opposite, in jumbo pasta shells.

Herbs in Butter

Butter is a real treat. That doesn't mean that you should routinely slather gobs of it on everything you eat, but when you want to put the finishing touches on a special dinner, go for butter every time. And not just plain butter: Blend into it your favorite combinations of herbs and other flavors.

Herb butters are simple and quick to make, and the flavor combinations and serving ideas are virtually unlimited.

MAKING BETTER BUTTER

Start with the freshest butter you can find. If you use unsalted butter you can control the amount of salt (if any) in the finished product, and its flavor is more delicate than that of the heavily salted varieties that are commonly available. Because butter is more perishable when unsalted, we recommend that you keep it frozen until you're ready to use it.

Any herbs or fruits to be used in the butter should be fresh but without excess moisture, which will hasten spoilage. If you are picking fresh herbs for use in butter, wash them in the garden, "on the hoof", the day before you cut them.

Choose herbs that complement each other as well as the dish you have in mind. Herbs with strong, earthy flavors blend well, as do those with more delicate flavors (see, for example, the Dill Burnet Butter opposite). Any herb blend you find pleasing is a good candidate for an herb butter. Do we all remember when mom dressed chickens with "poultry seasoning" that came out of a can and smelled divine? Now that we've grown up and can read the label, we can achieve that flavor in a basting blend with half a pound of butter, one or two pressed garlic cloves, a little salt and freshly ground pepper, and a teaspoon each of fresh chopped rosemary, lemon thyme, oregano, and sage.

You can use your food processor for blending herb butters, or you can mix them by hand if the ingredients are thoroughly chopped in advance. Begin with butter at room temperature, and thoroughly blend in the base ingredients—those that are powdery or pasty and others that add color and flavor but little texture. Then add the ingredients that are to be more apparent in the texture, such as herb leaves or olives.

Freshly made herb butter should be refrigerated for at least three hours (overnight is better) to allow the flavors to blend. It can be frozen as long as three months without noticeable loss of flavor.

SERVING SUGGESTIONS

You can pack your butters in ordinary plastic containers such as commercial margarine tubs or freezer containers, but it's more fun to do something fancy with them. Here are a few favorite ideas.

—Pack the butter into small plastic molds and freeze them, then pop each out into a plastic bag and keep frozen until served. Melt a molded shape of herb butter over fresh pasta.

—Roll butter into a fat cylinder, wrap it in plastic wrap, and chill it until solid. Slice off rounds as needed to top vegetables, fish, or bread.

—Pipe butter florets through a pastry bag fitted with a large star tip onto a cookie sheet, then freeze.

—Shave off colorful curls of refrigerated herb butter with a butter curler.

—Make butter balls with a melon baller, then add texture with butter paddles.

—With a rolling pin, roll the butter out about 1/4 inch thick, then cut various shapes with miniature cookie cutters. Freeze until ready to use.

—Whip the butter with a hand-held mixer until it is light and fluffy, then pack it in earthenware crocks. (You need a whisk attachment to whip butter in a food processor.)

—Use herb butter in making pastry crusts; use savory herbs for savory dishes and sweeter herbs (such as lavender and lemon verbena) for pastries.

BASIL GARLIC BUTTER

About 1 pound of butter

This butter can be made a pound at a time and frozen to use on the spur of the moment. For a picnic, you can grab a crock from the freezer, and the butter will be spreadable in a couple of hours.

1 pound unsalted butter at room temperature
Handful of fresh basil, clean and dry
2 to 3 cloves garlic
3 tablespoons parmesan cheese

Place the butter in a mixing bowl or the work bowl of a food processor. Put the garlic through a press into the butter. Add the cheese and whip with an electric mixer or process until the mixture is smooth and evenly blended.

Chop basil leaves fine and mix in, or add basil leaves and pulse until chopped to the desired consistency. Add salt to taste.

Pack butter into four crocks. Allow flavors to blend for at least 4 hours before serving. This herb butter can be frozen for about 3 months.

RED AND GREEN CHILE BASIL BUTTER

This is another versatile quick garnish to make something special of daily foods. It is good with beef, pork, chicken, and fish, either grilled or sautéed. It also enhances grilled eggplant, and grilled, roasted, or steamed potatoes and onions. When you have mature hot red peppers, such as hot cherry peppers, use them along with sweet green pepper. Either serranos or jalapeños are good as the hot green component paired with sweet red pepper.

1/4 pound unsalted butter, softened
1 tablespoon finely diced green pepper, either sweet or hot
1 tablespoon finely diced red pepper, either sweet or hot
3 tablespoons finely shredded basil leaves
1/8 teaspoon toasted and ground cumin

Mix all the ingredients together. Place the mixture on a sheet of waxed paper about 10 inches long. With the blunt side of a chef's knife, roll the butter into a compact cylinder.

Chill the butter until it is firm enough to cut easily. Divide the butter into 8 or 12 portions. Wrap the butter well in plastic wrap. For storage beyond 3 or 4 days, the butter may be frozen.

DILL BURNET BUTTER

This refreshing butter, with its hint of cucumber, is great served on grilled fish or fresh French bread with a salad. Choose young, tender leaves of burnet, as the older ones often are tough.

1/2 pound unsalted butter
1 teaspoon Dijon-style mustard
2 sprigs salad burnet (or more, to taste)
2 or 3 generous sprigs fresh dill
Blend all ingredients thoroughly until the mixture is pale green

SPICY BUTTER WITH FOUR PEPPERCORNS

Makes a generous 1/2 cup

The range of pepper flavors means that just a little of this butter adds a lot of taste. It is simple and easy to prepare, and goes with practically any dish, vegetable or meat, cooked in almost any style, whether steamed, boiled, sautéed, baked, or grilled. We like it especially with fish, poultry, potatoes, cauliflower, carrots, beets, squash, and corn. Wrapped tightly, it will keep in the refrigerator for up to a week, in the freezer for a month. If you prefer not to use pink peppercorns, (which may pose a slight health hazard), make a spicy butter with three peppercorns; replacing the teaspoon of pink peppercorns with equal amounts of green, white, and black.

1/2 cup unsalted butter, softened
1 teaspoon each of pink, green, white, and black peppercorns
1 garlic clove
2 to 3 tablespoons fresh minced parsley

Soften the butter in a small mixing bowl. Grind the peppercorns in a mortar and pestle to a medium coarseness; they should not be finely ground, but they shouldn't be too coarse either. Add them to the butter.

Mince the garlic or squeeze it through a garlic press and add to the butter along with the parsley. Blend all of the ingredients with a fork. Place the butter in a crock or small ramekin, cover with waxed paper or plastic wrap, and refrigerate for at least 1/2 hour before using.

Soup for all seasons

POTTAGE OF HERBS

Serves 4 to 6

1 cup each of dandelion greens, orach, lamb's-quarters,
watercress, skirrets (roots), and nettles, all fresh,
washed and chopped
1 bay leaf
1 tablespoon chopped fresh thyme
1 tablespoon chopped fresh parsley
1 onion, diced
1 small bunch fresh chives, chopped
1 teaspoon chopped fresh tarragon
Salt and pepper

Place all ingredients in a heavy saucepan with enough water to cover. Bring to a boil and simmer gently for about an hour. Cover and let stand 10 minutes. Remove bay leaf and serve with crusty bread or rolls and cheese.

PEPPER CREAM SOUP

Serves 4 to 6

This pretty pastel soup has a "what's in it?" subtlety. Increase the sweet peppers and add a few chiles for a spicier version.

3 tablespoons vegetable oil
1 cup chopped onion (1 large)
2 cups chopped red or green sweet pepper (2 to 3 large)
1 tablespoon fresh thyme, or 1/2 teaspoon dried
1 tablespoon chopped fresh marjoram, or
*   1/2 teaspoon dried*
2 cups chicken broth, preferably homemade
2 cups light cream
2 large eggs
Red or green pepper slivers, for garnish
Fresh thyme or marjoram sprigs, for garnish

Heat oil in a large saucepan over medium heat. Add onion and peppers and sauté until limp, about 5 minutes. Add herbs and cook 30 seconds more. Add broth and simmer, covered, until vegetables are very soft, about 20 minutes.

Strain soup; reserve liquid and puree solids in food processor or blender, leaving mixture not quite smooth for texture. Return puree to saucepan and stir in reserved liquid and cream.

Whisk eggs until broken up. Gradually add 1 cup of hot soup to the beaten eggs, whisking constantly. Return to pan. Heat but do not boil, or eggs will curdle! Ladle into warmed soup bowls and garnish with pepper slivers and herbs.

Pepper Cream Soup, recipe opposite.

FAVA BEAN SOUP WITH SAVORY

Serves 6 to 8

Favas, along with olives, are quintessential ancient Mediterranean foods. They are still important today in Italy, where they are mainly consumed as a green vegetable, and in the Middle East and North Africa, where the dried beans figure in soups, stews, and fritters. Favas have a tough outer skin which is rather bitter and indigestible except in very young beans. Therefore, the skins must be removed. The soup can also be made with canned fava beans or with any other white bean.

1 pound dried fava beans
6 large garlic cloves
1¹/₂ teaspoons toasted and ground cumin
2 teaspoons dried savory, or 2 tablespoons loosely packed
 fresh savory leaves
Salt and freshly ground black pepper
Garnishes: scallions, chopped fresh savory, fruity olive
 oil, lemon wedges

Soak the beans at least 24 hours in 4 quarts of cold water, then test a bean to see if the skin comes off easily. Starting with your thumbnail or a small sharp knife at the "waist" of the bean, peel a small section of skin up toward the small part of the bean. If the skin comes off fairly easily, you should be able to slip the bean out of its skin by squeezing it from the bottom. Soak another 12 to 24 hours if necessary, and discard any beans that can't be peeled.

Cover the beans with 4 quarts of cold water. Bring them to a boil, then immediately reduce heat to a simmer. Skim the liquid. Cook the beans for an hour. Add the garlic, cumin, and savory, then simmer for another hour. The beans should be very soft and melting into the broth. Puree the soup in batches in a food processor or blender. Season with salt and pepper.

The soup may be eaten immediately or, preferably, cooled to room temperature and then refrigerated overnight before serving. Serve it very hot. For garnish, thinly slice four or five scallions, including some of the green tops, and toss them with about a tablespoon of minced fresh savory leaves. Pass a cruet of fruity olive oil and a dish of lemon wedges along with the scallions and savory.

TARRAGON-MUSHROOM CONSOMMÉ

Serves 4

1 teaspoon fresh tarragon
1/4 pound diced mushrooms
1 rib celery, diced
1/2 cup diced carrot
1 large onion, peeled and diced
4 cups strong beef broth
1/4 cup dry sherry
Salt and pepper
4 cleaned, sliced fresh mushrooms

Simmer broth, onion, carrot, celery, diced mushrooms, and tarragon for 30 minutes. Strain out vegetables and tarragon. Add salt and pepper to taste, and simmer gently for 5 minutes to reheat. Serve garnished with fresh mushrooms.

POTATO HERBES DE PROVENCE SOUP WITH BUTTERED LEEKS

Serves 8

This creamy, comforting soup is a winter favorite; the addition of herbes de Provence lends a pleasant, subtle surprise.

1/4 cup butter
6 medium leeks (about 2 pounds), washed carefully,
 trimmed, and thinly sliced (white part only)
1/2 teaspoon salt
1/2 teaspoon sugar
1 tablespoon herbes de Provence
4 pounds potatoes, unpeeled and thinly sliced
4 cups chicken or vegetable broth
5 cups whole milk
2 scallions, thinly sliced

In a large soup pot, heat the butter over high heat until it foams. Turn heat to low, add the leeks, and sauté for 10 minutes, or until golden. Add the salt, sugar, and herbs and sauté 5 minutes longer. Add the potatoes and broth and bring to a boil. Reduce the heat and simmer for 45 minutes, stirring often, until the potatoes are tender. Puree the soup and return to the pot.

Add the milk and bring to a gentle boil. Simmer 10 minutes and serve, garnished with sliced scallions.

CHERVIL PURSLANE SOUP WITH LETTUCE

Serves 4 to 6

This soup is delicate but full-flavored, with a touch of refreshing tang provided by the purslane. It's especially good before grilled or broiled fish served with parsley and chive new potatoes.

2 tablespoons unsalted butter
2 tablespoons all-purpose flour
3 cups chicken broth
1/2 cup purslane leaves
1 cup chervil leaves
1 small head shredded leaf lettuce, such as butter or green leaf
1 cup half-and-half, at room temperature
Salt and freshly ground white pepper
Few sprigs chervil and purslane for garnish

Melt the butter in a medium-sized noncorrodible pot over low heat. Stir in the flour and cook over low heat for 5 minutes.

Add the chicken broth and stir well to combine. Cook over low heat for 10 minutes, stirring occasionally. Add the purslane and cook for 5 minutes. Add the chervil and lettuce and cook for 5 minutes.

Puree the herbs and vegetables in a blender and return them to the soup. Add the half-and-half and heat the soup over low heat until it is just hot, 2 or 3 minutes. Watch the soup carefully, as it can curdle if the heat is too high or if it is left too long over the heat. Season with salt and white pepper.

Serve the soup hot, garnished with chervil and purslane.

CORN SOUP WITH HERB CREAM

Serves 6

2 garlic cloves, minced
2 cups corn, fresh or frozen
3 cups chicken broth
1/2 cup chopped onions
1/4 cup grated carrots
1/4 cup chopped celery
1 1/2 teaspoons diced canned green chiles
1 cup low-fat milk

Combine all ingredients except milk in a saucepan, and bring to a boil. Reduce heat and simmer ten minutes. Puree in a blender or food processor, and strain through a sieve, pressing hard to extract juices from vegetables. Return to clean saucepan,

add milk, and simmer for 5 minutes. Serve with Herb Cream.

Herb Cream

2 tablespoons sour cream
1/4 cup nonfat yogurt
2 tablespoons chopped fresh parsley
2 tablespoons chopped fresh basil
1/2 tablespoon chopped fresh cilantro

In a blender or food processor, puree all ingredients until very well blended. Topping may be made one day ahead but must be stored in refrigerator.

At serving time, gently heat Herb Cream in a double boiler or microwave. Serve a spoonful in the center of each bowl of hot soup.

CRAB SOUP WITH LEMONGRASS AND COCONUT

Serves 6 to 8

Fresh lemongrass is as necessary to this dish as fresh basil is to pesto. If you cook the Dungeness crab or blue crabs yourself, steam them over plain water and do not season. Though the crab flavor will not be as pronounced, a pound of fresh, steamed and picked crab meat may be used. In this case, make the broth with chicken stock.

1 large steamed crab, such as Dungeness, 3 1/2 to 4 pounds, or 3 1/2 to 4 pounds steamed blue crabs
1 2-inch piece lesser galangal root, peeled, or 1 teaspoon rhizome (krachai) powder, or 1 1/2-inch piece ginger root, peeled
2 stalks (4 to 6 inches long) fresh lemongrass, outer leaves removed
3 shallots
2 garlic cloves
2 tablespoons Thai or Vietnamese fish sauce
1 teaspoon dried shrimp paste or 1/2 teaspoon anchovy paste
1 14-ounce can unsweetened coconut milk
1 green serrano chile, fresh
1 red serrano chile, fresh
2 Kaffir lime leaves, or zest of 1/2 lime
Juice of 1 lime, or to taste

Crack the crab shell and remove the meat in large pieces. Scrub the shells well and break them with a mallet or the blunt side of a chef's knife. Add the pieces to a food processor with 1 cup water and process for about a minute. Scrape the resulting mixture into a noncorrodible pan and add 4 cups water.

Hearty White Bean and Fall Greens Soup, recipe opposite, and Warm Cherry Tomato Surprise, recipe on page 50.

If you are using crab meat only, add 4 cups chicken stock to a noncorrodible pan.

Slice the galangal or ginger about 1/8 inch thick and add them to the shells and broth. Coarsely chop 1 stalk of lemongrass and add it to the pan. Coarsely chop 2 of the shallots and the garlic and add them to the pan. Simmer the broth for 15 minutes, skimming occasionally. Strain the broth into a clean, noncorrodible pan.

Stir the coconut milk very well and add half of it to the broth. Cut a 3-inch piece from the root end of the remaining lemongrass stalk and slice it into thin lengthwise slices. Finely dice the remaining shallot. Stem the chiles and slice them thinly on the diagonal. Remove the seeds if you wish. Add the lemongrass, shallot, chile, and Kaffir lime leaves or lime zest to the broth and simmer for 5 minutes. Add the crab meat and lime juice and heat through. Serve hot.

GREEN BEAN SOUP

Serves 4 to 6

This simple soup is a favorite. It is easy to make and is a good first course. Savory is a traditional bean herb; lovage adds an unexpected touch of spicy celery flavor.

6 cups chicken stock or 6 cups water and 4 teaspoons
* yeast-based chicken seasoning*
1 large onion, finely chopped
1 cup carrots, shredded
1 cup potatoes, diced
4 cups green beans, frozen or fresh
1 or 2 mild sausages, or 1/4 teaspoon hickory salt and
* a sprinkle of ground nutmeg*
1/2 teaspoon dried savory
1/2 teaspoon dried lovage
1 tablespoon fresh parsley, chopped
1/2 cup evaporated milk or half & half

Cook all ingredients except evaporated milk until beans are soft and other vegetables appear to be cooked. Add milk at the very last, and do not boil after adding it.

HEARTY WHITE BEAN AND FALL GREENS SOUP

Makes 6 generous servings

We find that old beans just won't become tender, no matter how you cook them, so use fresh dried beans in this hearty, very herbal autumn dish.

1 pound dried white beans, washed and picked over
1 large yellow onion, finely chopped
1 cup sliced celery
2 large cloves garlic, mashed
1 pound smoked Polish sausage (optional),
* cut in 1/2-inch dice*
4–6 sprigs each rosemary, sweet marjoram or
* oregano, sage, and thyme*
3–4 bay leaves
2 teaspoons ground coriander
8–10 cups poultry or vegetable broth, preferably
* unsalted, or water*
1 teaspoon salt
1/2 teaspoon freshly ground pepper
2 cups thinly sliced carrots
2 cups diced turnips or rutabagas
3–4 cups thinly sliced fresh greens, such as collards,
* Oriental cabbage, or turnip or mustard greens,*
* with tough stems removed*
1/4–1/2 cup robust herbal wine vinegar (see page 110)
1/4 cup chopped fresh parsley or other fresh herbs
* for garnish*

Place beans in a small roaster or Dutch oven and cover with water. Bring to a boil and cook for 5 minutes; turn off heat, cover, and let stand for an hour. Drain and rinse beans. Add onion, celery, garlic, sausage (if desired), herbs (except parsley), and coriander. Add enough broth or water to cover by at least 2 inches. Bring ingredients to a boil, reduce heat, and cover. Simmer over low heat about 1¼ hours, or until beans are nearly tender. Add more broth or water as needed to keep soup at about the same volume.

Add salt, pepper, carrots, and turnips. Continue cooking 25 to 30 minutes, or until vegetables are tender; add more liquid if desired. Add greens and cook about 10 minutes, or until just wilted. To thicken the broth, remove a spoonful of beans with a slotted spoon, mash or blend them, and return them to the pan. Stir in the vinegar; adjust salt and pepper as needed. Garnish with chopped fresh herbs just before serving.

Salads & herbal dressings

The Ultimate Herbal Salad

The tossed salad is in the midst of a culinary renaissance, thanks to health enthusiasts and herb epicures. A plethora of fresh herbs and leafy greens, a variety of vegetables and fruits, and an eclectic selection of tangy homemade herbal and fruit vinaigrettes are inspiring an array of new and exciting herbal variations on the humble salad.

For a long time, the tossed salad was a predictable and boring prelude to the main course: a lump of bland iceberg lettuce garnished with a wedge of tomato, topped with a few stale croutons and drowned in a puddle of turbo-caloried, additive-laced commercial salad dressing. In the past few years, people have begun to incorporate more leafy vegetables and herbs into their diet, and the tossed salad has undergone a much-needed transformation. Fragrant, leafy herbs such as cilantro, basil, mint, sorrel, watercress, and lemon balm have replaced imitation bacon bits, pebblelike croutons, and shredded synthetic cheese as salad enhancements, and even the salad foundation has changed.

GREENS

The main ingredient of a tossed salad, of course, is the lettuce. Years ago, the lettuce industry abided by the Henry Ford school of marketing: you could have any kind of lettuce you wanted as long as it was iceberg. Iceberg lettuce was ubiquitous but also the blandest and least nutritious of the lettuces.

The first demand of salad lovers was lettuces with more character. Then cooks concerned with flavor and texture began searching for heartier greens. (As a rule, the darker the leaf, the more nutritious and flavorful the salad.)

The selection of leaf lettuces appearing at the supermarket and farmer's market is growing. Red and green leaf lettuce, romaine, escarole, red oak leaf, and Boston bibb are a few of the varieties that offer texture, taste, and color. Tom Thumb butterhead, Buttercrunch, and lamb's ear are ideal varieties to grow at home. Leafy greens such as red and green swiss chard, spinach, curly endive, and kale also contribute toward a more robust salad.

Don't hesitate to mix two or three kinds of leaves together. Red swiss chard adds heartiness to a salad of romaine and green leaf lettuce. Mild-flavored sweet bibb lettuce benefits from the addition of sharply flavored escarole. Radicchio and red cabbage add vivid color, a slight bitterness, and a nice crunchiness.

Salad greens are easy to clean and prepare. Place the leaves in a colander set in a large bowl. Fill the bowl with cold water, covering the leaves. Mix the leaves around and then pull the colander out of the water and allow it to drain. Sand and dirt will remain in the bowl. Pat the leaves dry, shake off excess moisture, or whiz them in a salad spinner. (Leaves must be dry so that salad dressing will cling to them instead of making a pool on your plate.) Tear the leaves into bite-size pieces over a plate or bowl and gently toss them together with your fingers.

A variety of fresh herbs can be mixed with salad greens. Basil, sorrel, apple mint, spearmint, watercress, cilantro, and arugula are some favorites. Fresh tarragon and basil add sweetness; watercress and arugula provide a peppery bite. Sage, lemon balm, chive, and sorrel add softer but distinct flavors. Nasturtium and chive blossoms and opal basil contribute magnificent colors as well as palate-pleasing flavors.

Enhancements

The herbal salad is still growing, taking on a life of its own. For an easy, light, main-dish salad, add shredded carrots, vine-ripened tomatoes, sliced red onion or cucumber, mushrooms, and shredded monterey jack or colby cheese. Fresh fruit—chopped apples, pears, or plums—can be tossed in at the last minute. Walnuts, cashews, or almonds add crunch as well as protein.

Dressings

The salad is now ready to be dressed. There are plenty of commercial salad dressings on the market, packaged in fancy bottles and beckoning to be purchased. Leave them on the shelves. There's a whole world of homemade vinaigrettes waiting to be discovered and to cascade over your leafy creations.

Vinaigrette is the marriage of oil and vinegar. It is quick and easy to make, and unites the other salad ingredients. For a basic vinaigrette, all you need is a bowl and whisk or a jar with a lid to shake the ingredients together. You can tailor a dressing to your taste by adding a little vinegar for more tartness, or a little oil for a smoother finish.

Vinegar is commonly made from red or white wine, sherry, rice wine, apple cider, or champagne. Balsamic vinegar, which is aged longer and is less acidic than most vinegars, is superb but expensive. The growing interest in vinaigrettes benefits greatly from the many possibilities of flavored vinegars, created by steeping plain vinegar with a variety of fresh herbs, shallots, fruits, or peppers.

Because extra virgin olive oil contains a high percentage of mono-unsaturated fats, it is currently thought to be among the healthiest oils for a vinaigrette; its rich, fruity flavor adds character to any dressing. Soybean or safflower oil blended with olive oil is an adequate and less expensive substitute. Strongly flavored oils such as walnut, sesame, and avocado, used sparingly, add interest to delicate salads. As with vinegars, infusing oils with herbs is another way to add subtle flavor to the salad. Rosemary, thyme, tarragon, garlic, and marjoram are some favorites.

Herb-flavored vinaigrettes enhance a variety of other foods besides tossed salads. Turn roasted garlic potatoes in a vinaigrette and add rosemary, dill, and marjoram. Lightly dress a hearty salad of pasta, broccoli, tomatoes, red onion, and carrots. Or drizzle the vinaigrette over steamed asparagus, carrots, broccoli, or artichokes instead of butter or salt.

A dazzling variation on herb vinaigrette is the fresh fruit vinaigrette. The possibilities are almost endless: nectarines, plums, peaches, rhubarb, apricots, strawberries, raspberries, and blueberries, combined with a touch of fresh herbs and honey, are all excellent. And, besides adding a splash of color and flavor to salads, these velvety vinaigrettes can embellish asparagus, beets, carrots, or zucchini, enhance a fruit salad, or add zest to grilled chicken or pork. Fruit vinaigrettes require about half as much oil as most salad dressings.

Yogurt dressings are quick and healthful adornments to an herbal tossed salad. One favorite is a twist on the Indian condiment known as raita. Puree a peeled banana and cucumber, add them to about two cups of yogurt, and blend in mint, cilantro, or lemon balm. It's ideal for spicy meals that need cooling down or as a soothing dressing over bitter greens.

For a Middle-Eastern style dressing, add crunchy herbs such as rosemary, marjoram, oregano, or thyme to a dressing of about one cup tahini (a sesame seed paste), one cup yogurt, 1/4 cup lemon juice, and a few tablespoons of herbs. The tahini and yogurt dressing can serve as a dip for crudités as well.

Sample Salads

Herb and fruit vinaigrettes can enhance "theme" salads. For a tropical salad, add diced papaya, mango, pineapple, and shredded coconut to a base of leafy greens, along with refreshing leaves of spearmint or basil. A strawberry-mango or raspberry vinaigrette adds a zing of flavor and color. Tropical salads are ideal with grilled or broiled fish, chicken, or lean meat dishes.

For a Mediterranean salad, toss pasta spirals with herb vinaigrette, crumbled feta cheese, thyme, marjoram, parsley, oregano, cherry tomatoes, black olives, and chick peas. This is a nice accompaniment to shish kebabs and stuffed grape leaves, or convert it to an appealing dinner salad by adding cooked shrimp or chicken.

Many of these salads can be made ahead of time and packed for a picnic. For a summer stroll, bring along a simple Italian salad of chopped plum tomatoes, minced basil, garlic, oregano, mozzarella cheese, and pine nuts, accompanied by a loaf of bread. For an all-day jazz festival or ball game, a fruit salad of diced papaya, banana, Asian pear, and pineapple, tossed with a plum-nectarine vinaigrette, is a brilliant alternative to hot dogs and potato chips.

These are just a few of the possibilities; the variety of herbal salads is limited only by your imagination. Herbal salad bars may not be too far in the future. One thing is certain, however: once you discover the joys of herbal salads, the only tossing of iceberg lettuce you'll do will be tossing it out the window.

Spring Herb Salad

Serves 4 to 6

Here is a salad modeled on the classic English "sallets" of the sixteenth and seventeenth centuries. It is more restrained—ten or more herbs in a salad may be too many for the palate to comprehend: better to enjoy two different salads with five or six herbs each. Your garden is your guide to a spring salad. You may have the makings for an Italianate salad, with Italian parsley, tender marjoram tops, and rocket or basil thinnings, for example. To highlight the freshness of the salad, draw the thinnest veil of dressing over it.

6 to 8 sprigs tender salad burnet
6 to 8 sprigs tender tarragon tops
1 bunch watercress
8 to 10 small sorrel leaves
2 cups lamb's lettuce, or 1 small head butter lettuce
1/2 bunch chives, optional
About 1/2 tablespoon lemon juice, or mild white wine or fruit vinegar
Pinch salt
About 2 tablespoons pure olive oil
A dozen violets, pansies, or johnny-jump-ups, optional garnish

Remove any tough stems from the burnet, tarragon, watercress, and sorrel. Wash the greens and dry them. Cut the chives in 1-inch lengths and add them to the greens if desired.

Just before serving the salad, stir the lemon juice or vinegar with the salt to dissolve the salt. Toss the greens with the mixture. Sparingly add the olive oil until the greens are just coated.

Place the salad on a serving platter and garnish with violets if desired. Serve the salad immediately.

Dill Dressing

Makes about 1 cup

This dressing is offered as an example of how well dill combines with other herbs and how many foods it can complement. Try it with carrot and cabbage slaw, with green salad, beet salad, and composed salads containing raw fennel or steamed asparagus or cauliflower. It makes a delicious and different dipping sauce for steamed artichokes and gives new interest and flavor to chicken, fish, and meat salads—it's surprisingly tasty with canned tuna. You may substitute chervil or basil for the tarragon and garlic chives for the chives. Using an herb vinegar

Spring Herb Salad garnished with early violets, recipe opposite, and Borage Fritters with Capers, recipe on page 10.

containing the chosen herb heightens the flavor.

1½ tablespoons Dijon-style mustard
3 tablespoons white wine or herb vinegar
1/3 cup olive oil
1/3 cup chopped dill
1/4 cup chopped chives
Chopped leaves from 3 or 4 tarragon sprigs
Salt and freshly ground pepper

Mix the mustard with the vinegar in a bowl. Whisk in the olive oil, then stir in the dill, chives, and tarragon. Season with salt and pepper to taste. Add a little more vinegar or oil if you like.

HERB VINAIGRETTE

Makes a generous cupful;
easily doubled or quadrupled

This good, basic vinaigrette can easily be varied to suit individual tastes. Dried herbs can be used instead of fresh ones, but keep in mind that they are stronger, and you'll need less to flavor the vinaigrette. It will keep in the refrigerator for a week to ten days. Let it stand at room temperature for about 20 minutes before serving.

7/8 cup olive oil
2 tablespoons white wine vinegar or tarragon vinegar
1 teaspoon Dijon-style mustard
1/4 teaspoon salt, or to taste
Freshly ground black or white pepper to taste
Pinch sugar
1 medium clove garlic
1/2 cup packed fresh Italian parsley leaves
1 teaspoon packed fresh tarragon leaves or preserved
    tarragon leaves
1 tablespoon packed fresh basil leaves or 1 teaspoon dried
    basil leaves

Combine the oil, vinegar, mustard, salt, pepper, and sugar in a jar with a tight-fitting lid. Close the jar and shake vigorously until the vinaigrette is well blended.

Squeeze the garlic through a press, or mince it finely and add it to the jar. Place the fresh herbs on a cutting board and mince them finely; add them to the vinaigrette. If using dried herbs, crumble them into the vinaigrette.

Shake the jar again until the vinaigrette is thoroughly blended. Taste for seasoning; the vinaigrette is best if it stands for at least an hour before serving. Keep refrigerated.

The vinaigrette can also be prepared by adding all of the ingredients to a blender and blending them until smooth and homogeneous. This results in a lovely, bright green dressing that should be used within 5 days. It will separate after it has been refrigerated for several hours; just shake the jar to re-emulsify it.

PLUM-NECTARINE VINAIGRETTE

Makes 4 cups

This creamy, golden, tart-sweet dressing is delightful tossed with fruits or hearty greens.

4 plums, diced
3 nectarines, diced
1¼ cups vinegar
1/4 cup honey
1/8 teaspoon salt
1/8 teaspoon white pepper
3/4 cup olive or other vegetable oil
2 to 3 tablespoons fresh minced mint or basil

Place the plums, nectarines and vinegar in a nonreactive saucepan and cook for about 10 minutes over medium heat. Cool the mixture, first in the pan for 10 minutes, then in the refrigerator for about 30 minutes.

Add the fruit mixture, honey, and seasonings to a food processor fitted with a steel blade. Blend for 20 to 30 seconds or until the mixture is smooth. Slowly drizzle in the oil while the motor is running. Whisk in the herbs.

Serve the dressing immediately or refrigerate. If kept refrigerated, this vinaigrette should keep for about 1 to 2 weeks.

RASPBERRY VINAIGRETTE

Makes about 4 cups

Tangy raspberries lend an assertive flavor to this versatile dressing.

12 ounces raspberries
1 cup red wine vinegar
2 tablespoons Dijon-style mustard
1 teaspoon white pepper
1/2 teaspoon salt
2 to 3 tablespoons fresh minced cilantro, thyme, mint,
    basil, or arugula
2¼ cups olive or soybean oil

Whisk the raspberries, vinegar, mustard, seasonings, and herbs in a mixing bowl. Slowly drizzle in the oil while continuing to whisk. Use immediately or refrigerate; if kept refrigerated, the vinaigrette should keep for up to 2 weeks. Shake well before serving.

TARRAGON DRESSING

Makes 3/4 cup

This is particularly good with a salad of spinach, lettuce, sweet onions, and strawberries.

2 teaspoons to 1 tablespoon brown sugar
1/2 teaspoon fresh tarragon
1/4 teaspoon salt (optional)
1/2 teaspoon freshly ground black pepper
1/2 teaspoon paprika
1/4 teaspoon dry mustard
1/4 cup white wine vinegar
1/2 cup olive oil

Stir together herbs, spices, and vinegar. Whisk in oil until dressing emulsifies and appears creamy.

BUTTERMILK DRESSING WITH HERBS AND GREEN PEPPERCORNS

Makes about 1 1/2 cups dressing

This tangy dressing goes well with all kinds of salad greens and is especially good with cucumbers and summer-ripe tomatoes. Pour it over steamed and sliced new potatoes for a delicious warm potato salad. Coarsely crack the peppercorns in a mortar and pestle or use the flat side of a chef's knife to crack them on a cutting board. The dressing will keep, in a tightly covered jar, in the refrigerator for about a week.

2/3 cup buttermilk
1/3 cup olive oil
1 1/2 tablespoons lemon juice
1/4 cup mayonnaise
3 tablespoons garlic chives, snipped
1 teaspoon fresh minced tarragon
2 teaspoons cracked green peppercorns
About 1/2 teaspoon salt
1/4 teaspoon sugar

Whisk the buttermilk, olive oil, lemon juice, and mayonnaise in a small bowl until it is smooth and well blended. Blend in the remaining ingredients. Cover the bowl tightly with plastic wrap and refrigerate for at least 30 minutes. Correct seasoning and allow to come to cool room temperature before serving.

CHICKEN-MELON-MINT SALAD

Serves 6

2 chicken breasts
Chicken broth
3 medium cantaloupes
White wine
1/2 cup thinly sliced celery
1/2 cup macadamia nuts
1 cup green grapes, halved
1/2 cup fresh mint leaves, chopped
1/2 cup mayonnaise

Poach the chicken breasts in chicken broth, and let them cool in the broth. (This may be done a day ahead.) Cut the cantaloupes in half crosswise and scoop out the melon with a melon baller. Marinate the melon in white wine for at least four hours. Place melon halves upside down on paper towels to drain. Cut a thin slice from the bottom of each melon so that it will sit without rocking when placed upright.

When you are ready to make the salad, drain the chicken and pat dry. Shred the chicken rather than cutting it into chunks. Drain the melon balls. Lightly toss the chicken, melon, celery, nuts, grapes, mint, and mayonnaise until well mixed. Fill melon halves and garnish with a sprig of fresh mint. Serve with crackers.

ENDIVE AND RADICCHIO SALAD WITH BLUE CHEESE

Serves 4

This salad is very tasty—a lively blend of flavors and textures.

2 small Belgian endives, about 5 ounces
1 small radicchio, about 3 ounces
4 ounces blue cheese
1 small, ripe Bartlett pear, peeled and cored
3 ounces lightly toasted hazelnuts or pecans
1/3 cup fruity olive oil
1 tablespoon lemon juice, or to taste
2 tablespoons freshly grated or prepared horseradish
Salt and freshly ground pepper

Remove the outer leaves of the endive, setting aside 12 leaves. Remove the outer leaves of the radicchio, setting aside 4 leaves. Reserve these to garnish the plates. Chop the remaining endive leaves crosswise in little rounds. Tear or shred the radicchio leaves into bite-sized pieces. Combine them in a bowl with the blue cheese and toss lightly.

Quarter the pear lengthwise, then slice crosswise into 1/8-inch slices. Add the pear to the salad and cheese mixture. Coarsely chop the nuts.

In a small bowl whisk together the oil, lemon juice, horseradish, salt, and pepper. Taste for seasoning. Pour the dressing over the salad and toss lightly. On four salad plates arrange the reserved endive and radicchio leaves. Evenly divide the salad among the plates and garnish with the chopped nuts.

The salads may be chilled for up to 30 minutes, then brought to cool room temperature, or served immediately.

SPINACH AND WATERCRESS SALAD WITH BAKED HERBES DE PROVENCE CHÈVRE

Serves 6

Mild goat cheese baked in a crumb crust is a fine partner for crisp, dark greens; the addition of herbes de Provence takes it beyond the expected.

2 five- or six-ounce rounds of chèvre cheese, sliced
*   crosswise into thirds to make 6 rounds*
4 tablespoons olive oil
1/2 cup unseasoned dry bread crumbs
1 tablespoon herbes de Provence
1 bunch spinach (about 12 ounces)
1 bunch watercress (about 8 ounces)

Thoroughly coat the cheese rounds with oil. Mix the bread crumbs and herbs and press them all over the cheese rounds. Refrigerate, covered, for 1 hour. Wash, trim stems, and dry the spinach and watercress. Refrigerate until ready to use.

Dressing

1/2 cup olive oil
2 1/2 tablespoons balsamic vinegar
2 garlic cloves, minced
2 teaspoons Dijon-style mustard
1 teaspoon herbes de Provence
1/4 teaspoon salt
1/8 teaspoon white pepper
1 sweet red pepper, cut in strips

Combine all ingredients except the red pepper. Just before serving, bake the breaded chèvre rounds in an oven preheated to 400°F for 5 to 10 minutes, or until warm and softened. Combine the greens with the dressing and divide among six plates. Place the warm cheese rounds in the center of each plate and garnish with the red pepper strips.

SMOKED FISH SALAD WITH DILL VINAIGRETTE

Serves 4 to 6

This composed salad-appetizer can be made with any kind of smoked fish. Include two types—salmon for its color and flavor and any other kind that you have smoked or that is fresh-smoked from the market.

6 ounces smoked fish
12 baguette slices
1/4 cup extra-virgin olive oil
2 tablespoons white wine vinegar
1 shallot, finely diced
1/4 cup chopped dill
1 1/2 tablespoons nonpareil capers
Salt and freshly ground black pepper to taste
1 quart mixed small lettuces, cleaned and dried
Pickled onions for garnish (optional)

Slice the fish very thin. Toast the baguette slices until they are golden and crunchy and brush them lightly with olive oil while they are warm.

Whisk the remaining olive oil into the vinegar in a small bowl. Add the shallot, dill, and capers, and season with salt and pepper.

Arrange the fish slices on the toasted baguette croutons. Top each portion with about 1/2 teaspoon of the vinaigrette.

Toss the remaining vinaigrette with the lettuces and arrange the leaves on a platter. Arrange the croutons on the lettuce leaves and serve immediately, accompanied by pickled onions if desired.

WARM SPRING SALAD WITH THYME AND FETA VINAIGRETTE

Serves 3 to 4

This salad is a colorful first course or side dish. The vinaigrette also makes a light, versatile dressing for steamed vegetables, leafy greens, or grilled chicken. Serve with Thyme and Scallion Corn Muffins (see page 84).

1 large, fresh beet, peeled and cut into 2-inch-long
*   matchsticks*
12 asparagus stalks, halved
1 large carrot, cut into 2-inch-long matchsticks
1 cup Thyme and Feta Vinaigrette (see page 40)
4 or 5 leaves of lettuce (leaf or romaine)

Place the beet matchsticks in boiling water to cover and boil 6 to 8 minutes, or until soft. Drain and dis-

Smoked Fish Salad with Dill Vinaigrette, recipe opposite.

card the water. Place the asparagus in boiling water to cover and boil for 2 to 3 minutes. Drain and discard the water.

Toss together the beet, asparagus, and carrot in a mixing bowl. Arrange the mixed vegetables on a bed of lettuce, and spoon the vinaigrette over them. Serve warm as a first course or as a side dish with fish, chicken, or pasta.

Thyme and Feta Vinaigrette—*Makes 1 cup*

1/2 cup olive or vegetable oil
1/4 cup red wine vinegar
1/4 cup crumbled feta cheese
1 to 2 garlic cloves, minced
1 tablespoon Dijon-style mustard
2 tablespoons fresh thyme leaves, minced
1 tablespoon fresh marjoram, minced
1 tablespoon fresh oregano, minced
1 teaspoon honey
1/2 teaspoon white pepper
1/8 teaspoon salt

Place all ingredients in a jar, seal tightly, and shake vigorously for 10 seconds. Use immediately or refrigerate. Shake again before serving. If kept refrigerated, the vinaigrette should keep for up to 2 weeks. Serve with Warm Spring Salad (above) or with leafy green or chicken salads.

ORANGE AND CORIANDER SALAD

Serves 4 to 6

This salad is not for the timid! The combination of citrus, allium, and cilantro in various forms titillates the taste buds with every bite. We like this dressing, prepared with the optional zest, served with earthy spring vegetables: fresh steamed beets, new potatoes, and even asparagus.

1 head Boston or red leaf lettuce
1 cup cilantro
2 or 3 medium to large oranges
1 small red onion, sliced into thin rings
1/2 cup freshly squeezed orange juice
1/2 cup olive oil
1 small garlic clove
1/2 teaspoon coriander seed, toasted and finely ground
1 teaspoon orange zest (optional)
Salt and freshly ground pepper
Coriander flowers for garnish

Wash and pick over the lettuce, then tear it into large bite-sized pieces. Rinse the cilantro leaves, then spin or pat them dry with the lettuce. Peel the oranges and cut them in half lengthwise. Seed them if necessary, then cut them crosswise into 3/8-inch slices. Soak the onion rings in a bowl of cold water for 10 to 15 minutes.

Combine the orange juice and olive oil in a bowl or measuring cup. Put the garlic through a press into the dressing and add the ground coriander, zest, salt, and pepper. Blend well with a fork and taste for seasoning.

Drain the onions and squeeze or pat them dry. Arrange the lettuce and coriander leaves on a platter or salad plates. Place the oranges decoratively on top and scatter the onion rings over them. Cover the salad with coriander flowers and drizzle about half the dressing over it. Serve the salad immediately and pass the remaining dressing.

TWO TOMATO AND THREE BASIL SALAD

This simple concoction is great for the summer, when tomatoes and basil are in season. Use several types of tomatoes and basil, a combination of whatever looks good at the moment.

Large red tomatoes, quartered
Small pear tomatoes (yellow, if possible) or cherry tomatoes
Mild yellow or red onions, cut into strips
2 or 3 types of basil leaves (green leaf, anise, and lemon, for instance), clean and dry
Extra-virgin olive oil
Red wine vinegar, preferably homemade

Place quartered red tomatoes, onion strips, and whole small tomatoes in a dish with a cover.

Just before serving, dress the vegetables with olive oil and vinegar. (If you dress them too far in advance, they will become soggy and dull looking by mealtime.) Roll the fresh basil leaves into a cigar shape, then shred them with a sharp knife and sprinkle them over the tomatoes and onions. Toss and serve immediately.

ROCKET AND FRAISES DE BOIS SALAD

Serves 4 to 6

This lovely "gardener's special" salad deserves a place preceding or following an elegant spring dinner, especially if you have access to a crop of tiny, intensely flavored *fraises des bois* (Alpine strawberries).

It will draw many compliments, especially if served after a hot salmon mousse, and before a rich chocolate dessert.

2 large handfuls rocket (arugula, rucola) sprigs
1 pint fraises des bois, or substitute sliced ripe
  strawberries
3 tablespoons fruity olive oil
1 tablespoon raspberry vinegar
Pinch salt
Freshly ground white pepper to taste

Discard any tough stems from the rocket and wash and dry it. Wash the strawberries or *fraises des bois* carefully and remove the caps.

Arrange the rocket on a serving platter or individual plates, and scatter the berries over it.

Mix the olive oil and vinegar. Season lightly with salt and white pepper. Just before serving, whisk or shake to emulsify dressing, and drizzle it over the salad. Serve the salad immediately.

CONFETTI CORN RELISH

Serve this chilled as a condiment for grilled meats or chicken, or as a salad. It's appealing stuffed in tomato or red bell pepper halves or in whole, roasted and peeled poblano or Anaheim peppers.

1 red bell pepper, finely chopped
2 tomatoes, finely chopped
2 serrano chiles, finely chopped
1 red onion, finely chopped
1/4 generous cup fresh cilantro, finely chopped
2–3 tablespoons fresh epazote, finely chopped
1½ cups fresh corn, cooked, cut off cob, and chilled
3 cloves garlic, minced
4 tablespoons fresh lime juice
1/8 cup best quality olive oil
1/2 teaspoon cumin seeds, freshly ground
1/4 teaspoon allspice, freshly ground
1–2 small dried red chiles, ground
1 tablespoon gold tequila
1 tablespoon red wine vinegar
salt and pepper to taste
1/2 pound feta or montrachet cheese, crumbled

Mix all ingredients in a bowl except the cheese. Toss well and chill overnight. Serve garnished with the crumbled cheese and fresh cilantro sprigs and epazote leaves.

TOMATO AND CUCUMBER SALAD WITH BASIL FLOWERS

Serves 6 to 8

This dish is a great appetizer accompanied by a glass of wine and a crusty loaf of bread. It is best made with fresh imported mozzarella, but a domestic mozzarella will do.

2 medium ripe tomatoes
1 medium cucumber
1 medium sweet onion such as Vidalia, Walla Walla,
  or Texas
8 ounces mozzarella cheese
About 3 tablespoons olive oil
Salt and freshly ground pepper
1/3 cup basil flowers (or substitute 1/4 cup shredded
  basil leaves)

Core and chop the tomatoes into 3/4-inch dice. Peel the cucumber, quarter it lengthwise, and then cut it into 1/2-inch pieces. Cut the onion into 1/2-inch dice. Combine all the vegetables in a bowl.

Cut the cheese into 1/2-inch dice, or if using fresh mozzarella, shred it into bite-sized pieces. Add the cheese to the vegetables and toss.

Drizzle the oil over the vegetable mixture and season with salt and pepper. Toss the vegetables with the basil flowers and taste for seasoning. Add a bit more olive oil if the salad is not moist enough. Let the salad marinate at least 30 minutes, and as long as a few hours, before serving. Serve at cool room temperature.

Pasta, grains, & luscious legumes

Serves 6

The endless variety of polenta dishes cropping up on menus all over the country have taught us that cornmeal is not just for cornbread. The accent of basil is a delicious and colorful complement to the savory yellow polenta, and the rich, basil-studded mushroom sauce brings this simple dish up to the status of dinner-party fare.

3 cups water
1 cup cornmeal mixed with 1 cup water
4 garlic cloves, minced
1/4 cup chopped, fresh basil leaves
1/2 teaspoon salt
1/4 teaspoon white pepper
1 tablespoon butter
2 tablespoons freshly grated romano cheese
6 fresh basil sprigs

In the top of a double boiler, bring the 3 cups water to a boil. Add the wetted cornmeal, garlic, basil, salt, and pepper. Reduce heat and cook, stirring constantly with a whisk, until mixture comes to a boil. Place pan over boiling water and simmer for 15 to 30 minutes, stirring occasionally. Stir in butter and cheese. When butter is melted, remove polenta from heat, serve with Mushroom Sauce, and garnish with basil sprigs..

Mushroom Sauce

1 tablespoon butter
1 tablespoon olive oil
1/4 cup finely chopped onions
2 cloves garlic, minced
12 ounces mushrooms, cleaned and sliced
1 tablespoon chopped fresh basil

Heat butter and oil over medium-high heat in heavy pan. Add onions and garlic and sauté for 1 minute, stirring constantly. Add mushrooms and chopped basil and stir-fry, tossing to coat with butter mixture, for 3 minutes. Make a mound of polenta on each plate, and cover each mound with 1/6 of the Mushroom Sauce.

BAKED POLENTA WITH ITALIAN SAUSAGE, MUSHROOMS, AND THREE CHEESES

Serves 6 to 8

This is our idea of comfort food! Bland cornmeal needs a real shot of flavor, so don't hold back on the herbs. Adjust the seasoning to taste.

1 tablespoon fruity olive oil
1 small yellow onion, chopped
2 large cloves garlic, minced
1 medium red sweet pepper, cored, seeded, and chopped
1/2 pound mild Italian sausage (the kind with fennel seed and garlic) with casing removed
1/2 pound fresh crimini, button, or other mushrooms as available, trimmed and thinly sliced
$2^1/2$ cups milk, broth, or water
3/4 cup yellow cornmeal, preferably stone-ground
1 tablespoon chopped fresh sage
1 tablespoon chopped fresh Italian parsley
1/4 teaspoon ground cayenne pepper
1 cup skim- or whole-milk ricotta cheese
1/2 cup shredded gruyère or other swiss cheese
Salt and freshly ground black pepper to taste
4 tablespoons melted butter or margarine
4 tablespoons grated parmesan cheese
Fresh Tomato Sauce (recipe follows)
Chopped fresh Italian parsley and herb sprigs for garnish

Heat olive oil in a medium skillet; sauté onion, garlic, and sweet pepper until hot through. Add crumbled sausage and continue cooking just until meat changes color. Stir in mushrooms and cook until hot through. Drain excess fat and set mixture aside.

Place milk or other liquid in a large, heavy saucepan over moderately high heat; slowly add cornmeal, stirring briskly with a wire whisk to prevent lumping. Bring to a boil and cook 10 minutes, or until mixture is very thick and smooth; stir constantly to prevent scorching.

Remove pan from heat and stir in herbs, cayenne pepper, and ricotta and gruyère cheeses. Add sausage and sweet pepper mixture, combine well, then season to taste with salt and pepper. Pour mixture into two 9-inch pie plates lined with plastic wrap. Cool on a wire rack, then cover and refrigerate at least an hour, or as long as three days.

When ready to serve dish, preheat oven to 375° F. Cut polenta in wedges and place on an oiled shallow baking pan large enough to hold polenta in one layer without crowding. Drizzle with melted butter and sprinkle with parmesan cheese. Bake 15 to 20 minutes, or until polenta is lightly browned and very hot when tested with a small knife in center of wedge. Serve with Fresh Tomato Sauce (below), and garnish with chopped fresh parsley and sprigs of herbs.

Fresh Tomato Sauce—*Makes about 3 cups*

2 tablespoons extra-virgin olive oil
1 medium yellow onion, finely chopped or thinly sliced
2 large cloves garlic, peeled and mashed
$2^1/2$ pounds ripe fresh tomatoes or imported canned tomatoes, drained and cut in 1/2-inch dice; reserve juice
2 teaspoons chopped fresh rosemary
2 teaspoons chopped fresh sage
1 tablespoon chopped fresh parsley, preferably flat-leaved
1/2–3/4 cup dry white wine
Salt and freshly ground black pepper

Heat olive oil in a large skillet over moderately high heat; sauté onion and garlic until softened. Add tomatoes gradually, keeping heat as high as possible without browning. Stir in herbs, wine, and any reserved tomato juice; reduce heat to low and simmer for about 20 minutes, or until vegetables are softened and fragrant. Add more wine or water if needed to prevent sticking and maintain desired consistency. Season with salt and pepper to taste.

GOLDEN SAFFRON RICE

Serves 12

3/4 cup butter
1/4 teaspoon cayenne pepper
1/2 teaspoon saffron
1 tablespoon salt, or to taste
3 cups brown or converted white rice
6 cups water or chicken broth
3/4 cup cashews, broken
1 tablespoon sweet marjoram, chopped
1/4 cup parsley, chopped
1/3 cup lemon juice

If saffron is in thread form rather than powdered, toast it in a small heavy skillet over medium heat until it is crisp and begins to darken. Cool and powder it with a pestle or back of a spoon.

Place butter, cayenne, saffron, salt, and water in saucepan and bring to a boil. Add rice. Return to a boil. Reduce heat and cover. Cook 20 to 25 minutes for white rice, 35 to 40 minutes for brown.

Just before serving, add cashews, marjoram, parsley, and lemon juice. Stir with a fork until well mixed.

Note: Leftover rice makes excellent salad—add extra nuts, and green vegetables for color. Toss with oil and lemon juice dressing.

RISOTTO WITH SEAFOOD AND DILL

Serves 6 to 8

This dish is very Italian, with clean, definite seafood, herb, and rice flavors and a creamy broth that bathes the rice. Cheese is optional; though seldom served with seafood in Italy, cheese seems to be an American preference in rice and pasta seafood dishes. Feel free to substitute other shellfish or finfish. Italians frequently serve small shellfish in the shell in risotto and with pasta, and the effect is quite attractive. If you cannot find scallops in the shell, use shelled scallops and sauté them with the shrimp.

1 pound medium shrimp, 16–24 count
2 to 3 pounds assorted bivalves in the shell, such as
    Manila clams, small mussels, and scallops
1 cup dry white wine
water
1 bunch dill
1 small onion, diced fine
1 bay leaf
1 quart fish broth or 16 ounces bottled clam juice
3 tablespoons olive oil
2 tablespoons unsalted butter
1 small onion, chopped coarse
2 or 3 garlic cloves, minced
2 cups arborio rice
3 or 4 green onions, trimmed with about
4 inches green and cut in 1/2-inch lengths (optional)
Salt and freshly ground pepper to taste
Lemon wedges (optional)
About 1 cup freshly grated parmesan cheese (optional)

Shell and devein the shrimp, rinsing only if necessary. Reserve the shells to enhance the broth.

Heat the other shellfish, one kind at a time, in the wine in a tightly covered pan. Remove them to a dish as they open.

Strain the shellfish liquor into a pot through a sieve lined with rinsed white paper toweling or tripled cheesecloth. Add the shrimp shells, about 2 cups of water, three or four dill sprigs, the coarsely chopped onion, bay leaf, and fish broth or clam juice. Simmer about 15 minutes, then strain and measure the broth. You should have at least 2 quarts; add wine or water if necessary to equal this amount. Add salt and pepper to taste. Heat the broth to just below a simmer and keep warm.

Meanwhile, sauté the shrimp in 1 tablespoon of olive oil for about 1½ minutes, or until just pink. Transfer the shrimp to the dish with the other shellfish.

Place the remaining olive oil and the butter in a large casserole that can be used on the stove, cover, and sweat the diced onion and the garlic over medium-low heat. When the onion is softened, add the rice, stir well, and reduce the heat. Sauté the rice gently for about 10 minutes, then stir in about 2 cups of broth. Raise the heat again to medium-low. Continue stirring the risotto and adding more broth, about 1/2 cup at a time, as soon as the previous addition of liquid has been absorbed.

Meanwhile, remove the leaves from five or six dill sprigs and chop them.

The risotto will be creamy and the rice al dente when it is done, in 16 to 20 minutes. Two or three minutes before this point, stir in the bivalves, then the shrimp, chopped dill, and green onions if desired. When the dish is heated through, remove it from the heat and add salt and pepper. If the risotto is too thick, add more hot broth. Serve immediately. Pass lemon wedges and cheese if desired.

LEMON BASIL VERMICELLI

Serves 8

12 ounces vermicelli
1 cup scallions, chopped
1 cup lemon basil, chopped
1/2 teaspoon black pepper
3 tablespoons fresh lemon juice
2 tablespoons soy sauce (light, if available)
5 drops hot chile oil (or more, to taste)
2 teaspoons corn oil
2 teaspoons oriental sesame oil

Boil vermicelli in a large pot of water and drain well. Toss vermicelli with scallions, lemon basil, pepper, lemon juice, soy sauce, and hot chile oil. In a wok or large frying pan, heat the corn oil with the sesame oil over medium heat. Stir-fry vermicelli mixture in the hot oil for five minutes, tossing often to prevent sticking. Serve under or with Anise Baby Squash Orientale (see page 53).

Risotto with Seafood and Dill, recipe opposite.

VEGETABLES AND LINGUINI ON A BED OF ARUGULA AND RADICCHIO

Serves 6

1 15-ounce can white beans, drained
1/2 cup chopped celery
1 cup chopped jicama
1/4 cup chopped green bell pepper
1/4 cup chopped red bell pepper
1/4 cup chopped yellow bell pepper
1/4 cup chopped onions
1/4 cup grated carrot
2 garlic cloves, minced
2 tablespoons minced fresh rosemary
1 tablespoon minced fresh mint
2 tablespoons white wine
1½ tablespoons olive oil
3 tablespoons fresh lime juice
2½ tablespoons chicken broth

1 tablespoon sugar
1 teaspoon ground cumin
1/4 teaspoon white pepper
1/4 teaspoon salt
6 ounces linguini
3 ounces arugula
3 ounces radicchio (other greens may be substituted for arugula and radicchio)

Combine all ingredients except linguini, arugula, and radicchio, and toss well. Marinate several hours or overnight. Cook linguini in a large pot of boiling water and drain well. Run under cold water and drain again. Set aside. Wash arugula and radicchio and store in refrigerator. At serving time, divide arugula and radicchio among six plates. Place one-sixth of the linguini on top of the greens. Drain the vegetables, reserving marinade. Place the vegetables on top of the pasta, and drizzle on the marinade. Serve immediately.

Herbs with Beans—A Harmonious Marriage

Beans taste good any time of the year, but when there's a nip in the air and the leaves begin to turn, they really come into their own. To our minds, there is no more welcome dish on a cold winter day.

Cooking beans well is a fine art, and herbs have everything to do with it. Almost nowhere else in cooking do herbs make such a difference. Most beans are bland; they readily take on the flavor imparted by herbs, which can transform a dish from ordinary to memorable.

There are some 400 named varieties of beans, and their history is long. Evidence of legumes (the family to which beans belong) has been found in the lake dwellings of Switzerland and the tombs of ancient Egypt, and they were widespread in North and South America long before Europeans arrived.

Beans and other legumes are easy to grow; most don't need nitrogen fertilizers and, in fact, are self-contained fertilizer factories. Nitrogen-fixing bacteria, living in root nodules, convert atmospheric nitrogen into compounds the plants can use, then store them in the nodules. When the bean plants die or are plowed under, they decompose, and the nitrogen compounds become available to the next plants that grow there. Some varieties of beans will grow well in exceedingly dry areas.

Many of us have experience with beans that goes back to our childhoods growing up during the Depression. Of course, everyone ate lots of beans; they were cheap, available, and filling. Into the bean pots went lots of onions and a hefty hunk of slab bacon, rind intact. Those beans simmered all day, and the air was filled with the goodness of their aroma.

Beans have long been known as the food of the poor in cultures worldwide, but recently they have become trendy. And why not, in this age of diet consciousness? They're an inexpensive and healthy source of many nutrients, including protein, and they're high in cholesterol-reducing fiber, which also fills empty stomachs. The complex carbohydrates in beans are digested slowly and provide a constant and even source of energy.

COOKING BEANS

It's not necessary to take the day off to prepare a bean dish. Beans are adaptable and, with a little planning, can easily fit into a busy schedule. Beans can simmer in an electric crockpot while you're away, or you can cook large amounts and freeze them in meal-sized containers, ready to thaw when you need them.

Doneness is important. Beans should not be too firm and resistant, nor should they be mushy and shapeless except in soups or purees. Start out with a good long soak, up to 12 hours, then drain and replace the water before firing up the stove. This is especially important at high altitudes, where beans have been known to remain firm through days of cooking. However, if you really are short of time or have forgotten to soak the beans, there is a quick alternative. Cover the beans with water and bring to a boil, then remove from heat and let sit, covered, for one hour. Drain and replace the water to at least 1½ inches above the beans, then begin cooking. Keeping the lid on will speed the heating of the water, and once the pot is boiling, reduce heat to a slow simmer, leaving the lid on to prevent too much of the cooking water from escaping prematurely. Don't add any acidic ingredients or salt until a bean can be easily crushed between your tongue and the roof of your mouth, as these will slow the cooking process.

The choice of a cooking pot is important, too. Aluminum is not recommended. Enamelware or stainless steel are fine, but the best pot by far is a well-seasoned iron kettle. It seems to transfer heat much better than the thinner, lighter-weight pots, it adds a small amount of iron to food that's cooked in it, and besides, it feels good to cook with it.

FLAVORING BEAN DISHES

Certain herbs have an affinity for certain foods, and beans are definitely a case in point. Savory (winter or summer), possibly one of the least used of the common culinary herbs in the United States, has long been known as the "bean herb" in Germany, and in my house the bean pot always gets at least a little bit. Cumin puts a little magic in bean dishes, imparting a distinctively Mexican or Indian aura (depending on the other ingredients). Bay leaves establish a subtle, solid flavor base when added during the initial cooking stages; they should be removed before serving. Parsley is always welcome: it contributes more to looks than to flavor, but visual appeal is a powerful appetite stimulant. We almost always add oregano, though more than 1/2 teaspoon of dry herb can be overpowering in some dishes. Cilantro, or fresh coriander leaf, is the same way; a lot can be too much, and some people dislike it altogether, but a little (perhaps a teaspoon of fresh herb) is indispensable. It adds a coolness and freshness that seem to round out other flavors.

For beans cooked Italian style, as in minestrone, basil and fennel are excellent, and basil is good in bean dishes containing a lot of tomatoes. Otherwise, though, we don't generally use these herbs in bean dishes.

Onions go well in almost everything, and they always give a flavor boost to beans. Garlic is another addition that's difficult to resist, even if only a clove or two. Lovage, Mexican oregano (*Lippia graveolens*), and epazote are interesting herbs to experiment with if you have them handy, and a hint of ground cloves can impart a Spanish influence. A dash of vinegar or lemon juice seems to bring out the other flavors, and the merest sprinkle of Tabasco adds a zesty note.

Most herbs should be added at the beginning of cooking so that the flavors will blend. Toward the end, after a taste, more herbs can be added if needed. Cilantro goes in at the very last, though; its flavor is better if it's not overcooked, and the beautiful bright green pleases the eye. And if you are using basil, try adding some at the beginning and more at the end of cooking.

Ham hock or salt pork have long been used to give bean liquor a flavorful richness. But vegetarians and those who are limiting fats must rely on something other than meat to create that effect. The herbs do much in this direction. Most commercial bouillons are too salty and laced with questionable ingredients, and you should shy away from them, though some of the yeast-based chicken- and beef-flavored seasonings are okay. Miso, a fermented soy paste, adds a fine richness and flavor to bean broth, and extra vegetables—particularly onions, celery, and carrots—can do wonders. You could also add just a sprinkle of hickory salt or liquid smoke, or a couple of tablespoons of roasted sesame oil, as a substitute for the smoked flavor sometimes found in ham-flavored bean dishes.

Experiments with herbs in beans can hardly go wrong and ruin a dish if you begin with small amounts of each herb, taste often, and gradually increase the amounts as you learn the different flavors. The balance of herbs should be part of your experiments; increasing the amount of just one herb in a blend can entirely change the effect, and the same blend will react differently with different beans and other ingredients. With experience, as they say in India, "The hand knows."

STEWED BLACK BEANS

Black beans are very flavorful, and this stew is thick and hearty—perfect for the main course on a nippy winter's night.

2 cups black turtle beans, soaked
4 cups water
1 medium onion, chopped
1 rib celery, chopped
2 cloves garlic, mashed
1/2 green pepper, chopped
1/2 cup crushed tomatoes (available canned)
1 tablespoon roasted sesame oil (optional)
1 tablespoon miso paste
1 tablespoon lemon juice
1 teaspoon dried oregano
1/2 teaspoon crushed cumin
Dash of Tabasco
1 tablespoon rum (optional)
Salt and pepper to taste
1 tablespoon fresh parsley
1 tablespoon fresh cilantro

Bring beans and water to a boil and add all ingredients except tomatoes, rum, lemon juice, parsley, and cilantro. Simmer until beans are soft, about 1½ to 2 hours. Add crushed tomatoes, rum, and lemon juice and cook another 30 minutes. Leave the lid off during this time to reduce and thicken the liquid.

Remove 1 cup of the bean mixture, whir in blender or mash thoroughly, and return to pot. Just before serving, sprinkle with chopped cilantro and parsley.

SPLIT PEAS AND RICE

1 cup yellow split peas
3 cups water
1 small zucchini squash, diced
1 medium onion, chopped
2 ribs celery, chopped
1 carrot, chopped
1 clove garlic, mashed
1 tablespoon yeast-based chicken seasoning
1/2 teaspoon crushed cumin
1/2 teaspoon dried oregano
1 tablespoon each fresh cilantro and parsley
1/2 cup feta cheese, crumbled

Put all ingredients except cheese, cilantro, and parsley into a large saucepan, bring to a boil, and cover. Cook for about 30 minutes or until peas are somewhat soft but not mushy. There should be very little liquid left. Add a few drops of Tabasco sauce and taste to adjust seasonings. This is a matter of judgement, but the dish is better if the peas don't lose their shape.

Serve the split pea mixture over cooked brown rice and top it with the feta cheese and finely chopped parsley and cilantro.

HERBAL BEAN SAUSAGES

Makes about 20 one-inch sausages

These plant-based sausages taste great, contain no added fat unless you fry them in oil, and are easy to make. These ingredients yield fairly mild sausages; after you've tried them, adjust the seasonings to please your palate.

2 cups cooked pinto beans, mashed
1/2 cup whole wheat breadcrumbs
1/2 cup onion, minced
1 clove garlic, minced
1/2 cup tomato sauce
1/8 teaspoon fennel seed, crushed
1/8 teaspoon dried red pepper
1/8 teaspoon dried or 1/2 teaspoon fresh basil
1½ teaspoons chopped fresh parsley
Salt to taste

Combine all ingredients in a mixing bowl, mix thoroughly, and shape into 1- or 2-inch sausages. For maximum flavor and no added fat, place in a baking pan and broil, turning when edges are slightly crisp. Serve with Mushroom-Red Pepper Sauce below.

Mushroom-Red Pepper Sauce—*Makes about 1 cup*

1 red bell pepper, minced
1/8 to 1/4 cup vegetable broth or water
4 large mushrooms, minced (about 1/4 cup)
1/4 cup onion, minced
Salt to taste
1/8 teaspoon celery seed
1/2 teaspoon chopped fresh oregano
Dash black pepper
Whole wheat flour (pastry flour works best)

Cook red pepper in vegetable broth for 5 to 7 minutes or until tender. Add mushrooms, onion, salt, celery seed, oregano, and black pepper. Cook 5 minutes longer or until onion is transparent. Quickly whisk in enough flour to just thicken the sauce, about 2 tablespoons at a time. Immediately remove from burner. Do not overcook, or flour will cake. If needed, add more vegetable broth or water. Serve over sausages, whole grains, or vegetables.

White Beans with Herbes de Provence Cream

Serves 8

This rich, flavorful bean dish is a hearty vegetarian entree or an assertive accompaniment for roast lamb. The Herbes de Provence Cream provides a perfect finish.

1 pound dried white beans
2 tablespoons vegetable oil
2 cups chopped onions
6 garlic cloves, minced
2 tablespoons herbes de Provence
7 cups chicken or vegetable broth
2 cups chopped fresh tomatoes
1 cup chopped fresh parsley
1/4 teaspoon white pepper

Soak the beans overnight in water to cover (or bring beans and water to a boil, turn off the heat, and soak, covered, 1 hour). Drain.

Heat the oil in a heavy pot over medium heat. Add the chopped onions and sauté 5 minutes, stirring frequently. Add the garlic and herbes de Provence and sauté 5 minutes, stirring. Add the soaked beans, broth, tomatoes, parsley, and pepper and bring the mixture to a boil. Simmer for 2 hours, or until the beans are tender. Serve hot, topped with Herbes de Provence Cream.

Herbes de Provence Cream

1/2 cup chopped scallions
1¼ cups sour cream
1 tablespoon herbes de Provence
1/4 teaspoon salt
1/4 teaspoon white pepper

Mix all ingredients and place a spoonful on top of each portion of beans just before serving.

Frijoles Negros in Olla (Black Beans Cooked in a Clay Pot)

Serves 6 to 8

One of our favorite meals is a bowl of thick, musky black beans seasoned with chiles, oregano, and hoja santa and balanced with the pungency of epazote. Cooked down until thick, the beans may be served in bowls garnished with chopped green onions, freshly chopped cilantro, sour cream or crumbled goat cheese, and lime wedges.

1 pound dried black beans
Water or broth to cover beans by about 1½ inches
3 tablespoons olive oil or bacon fat
1 whole onion, quartered and studded with 2 cloves
4–6 whole garlic cloves
1/2 teaspoon cumin seeds
1/2 hoja santa leaf, torn into several pieces
1–2 whole dried red chiles (ancho or pasilla or New Mexico ristra *chiles)*
Salt to taste
1 teaspoon dried Mexican oregano
3 sprigs fresh epazote

Wash beans well. Cover with water or broth. Add oil, onion, garlic, and cumin. Brring to boil; reduce heat, adding the hoja santa and the dried chiles, and simmer for approximately 2½ hours. Should too much water evaporate, add hot water to prevent beans from bursting. When almost tender, add the salt, oregano, and epazote, and cook for another 15 minutes. When beans are tender, the liquid should just cover them; too much liquid will give a watery broth.

Vegetables, plain & fancy

WARM CHERRY TOMATO SURPRISE

Serves 6 to 8

We first tasted this dish long ago on a balmy summer evening at a restaurant by a lake in Bucharest, Romania. The waiter whispered, "The surprise is the bite of the hot pepper."

1¹/₂ pounds ripe cherry tomatoes
1–2 mildly hot fresh green chiles (Anaheim, New Mexican, poblano, or wax type)
1 large clove garlic, peeled and mashed with 1/2 teaspoon salt
2–4 tablespoons olive oil, or enough to lightly coat tomatoes
2 tablespoons chopped fresh sage
1/2 cup crumbled feta cheese
Crusty French or Italian bread, sliced and brushed on both sides with olive oil
Salt and freshly ground black pepper to taste
Italian parsley and whole sage leaves for garnish

Preheat oven to 300°F. Cut cherry tomatoes in half if large. Place in a large bowl and add sliced chiles. Combine olive oil, garlic, and sage in a small bowl; pour over tomatoes and add cheese. Toss gently to avoid breaking up tomatoes. Season with salt and black pepper to taste. Place tomato mixture in a large, shallow pan and warm in oven for 20 minutes until fragrant and hot through.

While tomatoes are baking, toast or grill bread on both sides until golden. Serve with warm tomatoes piled on toasted bread. Garnish with chopped parsley and sage leaves.

ROSEMARY GLAZED CARROTS

Serves 3 or 4

12 long, thin carrots, peeled but not cut
1/4 to 1/3 cup rosemary honey (steep several sprigs of fresh rosemary in a light-flavored honey for a week or more)
2 tablespoons butter
Sprig of fresh rosemary

Cook carrots in boiling water to cover until they are tender but firm. Meanwhile, warm the honey and butter just enough to melt the butter and allow thorough blending. Drain the water from the carrots and toss them in the honey mixture. Mince a small amount of fresh rosemary and sprinkle it lightly over the dish.

VEGETABLES A LA GRECQUE

Serves 6

Though we don't know why this preparation is called Greek-style, we suspect the idea came from Cyprus, where many vegetables are cooked with abundant coriander seed. Mushrooms, cauliflower, and broccoli are also good when pickled in this manner. Choose a total of two pounds of your favorite vegetables. Large artichokes may be used; they will take longer to cook. The marinated vegetables will keep for a week or so in a tightly closed container in the refrigerator.

Court Bouillon

2 tablespoons lightly toasted coriander seed
1 bay leaf
2 or 3 Italian parsley sprigs
1 or 2 thyme sprigs
Juice of 1 large lemon, strained
1 teaspoon salt
1 teaspoon peppercorns
4 cups water

Vegetables

6 to 8 baby artichokes, about 1/2 pound
1/2 pound small carrots, peeled and trimmed
2 or 3 tender inner celery ribs, washed and trimmed
1/2 pound small zucchini and/or crookneck squash,
    washed and trimmed
Garnish: 2 or 3 tablespoons fruity olive oil

Bring the court bouillon ingredients to a boil, then reduce heat and simmer for 15 minutes. Strain and return to pan.

Prepare the vegetables while the court bouillon is cooking. Trim artichokes of tough outer leaves and stems. If the artichokes are large, trim to the hearts, remove chokes, and cut into quarters or sixths. Halve baby artichokes lengthwise and remove chokes. Place prepared artichokes in a bowl of acidulated cold water. Wash, trim, and cut the remaining vegetables into pieces of an even size.

Carrots and celery will take 12 to 15 minutes to cook; artichokes, 10 to 12 minutes; cauliflower, 6 to 8 minutes; and summer squash, mushrooms, or broccoli, 4 to 5 minutes. Simmer the vegetables in the court bouillon until they are firm-tender. Let them cool to room temperature in the court bouillon. Remove and serve at cool room temperature. Just before serving, garnish with a little flavorful olive oil. If you wish more pickle-like vegetables, cover them tightly and store them in the refrigerator for 3 or 4 days before serving.

GARLIC-OLIVE OIL POTATOES WITH FRESH ROSEMARY

Serves 6

These potatoes are so simple to prepare, they have no right to taste as fabulous as they do. Even with such a small amount of oil, the potatoes have a crispy coating and are permeated with the flavor of garlic and fresh rosemary.

6 medium red potatoes (about 1 1/2 pounds)
1 tablespoon olive oil
1/4 teaspoon salt
1/8 teaspoon white pepper
2 tablespoons fresh rosemary
3 large cloves garlic, peeled and sliced

Place potatoes in a baking dish just large enough to hold them in a single layer. Drizzle potatoes with olive oil, shaking the pan so the oil coats all surfaces of potatoes. Sprinkle with salt, pepper, and rosemary, again shaking the pan to coat the potatoes thoroughly. Place garlic slices on and between potatoes. Bake in a preheated 400°F oven for 40 minutes, or until tender when pierced with a knife.

SUPER SIMPLE SQUASH WITH SAGE

1 pound of squash serves 3 to 4

It hardly gets simpler than this, and the mild flavors of the cheese and squash let the fresh sage flavor shine through.

Zucchini or yellow squash, sliced lengthwise in
    1/4-inch pieces
Shredded cheese: cheddar, muenster, monterey jack,
    or mozzarella
Thinly sliced fresh sage leaves

Preheat oven to 450°F. Place squash slices on a lightly oiled shallow pan and bake about 10 minutes, or until slices look dry and are beginning to be tender. Reduce temperature to 350°F and remove squash from oven. Layer the slices in a shallow casserole with cheese and sage leaves, ending with cheese. Bake until cheese is melted and dish is heated through. Garnish with sage leaves and serve immediately.

Anise Baby Squash Orientale, recipe opposite, on Lemon Basil Vermicelli, recipe on page 44.

ANISE BABY SQUASH ORIENTALE

Serves 8

2 pounds assorted baby summer squash such as zucchini,
crookneck, and patty pan, or use regular-size squash
cut in pieces
2 tablespoons chicken broth
1 tablespoon rice wine vinegar
1/2 tablespoon soy sauce
1 tablespoon Chinese oyster sauce
1/2 tablespoon cornstarch
1 tablespoon water
3 tablespoons anise basil, chopped

Slice and steam the squash just until fork-tender.
Gently heat broth, vinegar, soy sauce, and oyster
sauce together in a medium-size saucepan. Toss the
hot steamed vegetables with the broth mixture, and
place pan over high heat. When the liquid boils, stir
in cornstarch mixture. Turn heat to low and gently
toss vegetables to coat with sauce. Sprinkle with the
basil and serve over or with Lemon Basil Vermicelli
(see page 44).

CAULIFLOWER WITH LEMON-TARRAGON MAYONNAISE AND CHEESE CRUST

Serves 6

The textures and flavor combinations in this dish
make it a winner. The cauliflower is covered with a
crust of cheddar cheese over a creamy mayonnaise
sauce accented with lemon, Dijon-style mustard,
and tarragon.

1 medium head cauliflower (about 1½ pounds)
1/3 cup mayonnaise
1 teaspoon fresh lemon juice
1/2 teaspoon grated lemon zest
2 teaspoons Dijon-style mustard
1/8 teaspoon white pepper
2 tablespoons minced tarragon
1 cup (about 2 ounces) grated cheddar cheese

Steam whole head of cauliflower for 15 minutes,
until barely done. Cool slightly. Combine mayonnaise, lemon juice and zest, mustard, pepper, and
tarragon. Spread mayonnaise mixture over cauliflower. Pat cheese onto mayonnaise-coated head of
cauliflower and bake in a preheated 350°F oven for
10 minutes. Cool for a few minutes to let cheese set,
and slice into 6 wedges.

PARSNIPS WITH NUTMEG AND PARMESAN

Serves 6

The natural sweetness of parsnips is enhanced by
nutmeg. Substitute mace if you like, or a combination of the two spices. These are a good accompaniment to roast chicken, lamb, or beef, especially if
the meat has been flavored with rosemary or thyme
and garlic.

2 pounds parsnips
6 tablespoons unsalted, melted butter
1/3 cup freshly grated parmesan cheese
1/2 teaspoon freshly grated nutmeg, or to taste
Salt
1 cup all-purpose flour
4 tablespoons unsalted butter

Peel and core the parsnips, and julienne the flesh.
Cook the parsnips in lightly salted boiling water
(enough to cover) until they are tender, 5 to 10 minutes. Cooking time for parsnips varies considerably,
depending on how long they were in the ground before harvest and on storage conditions after harvest. They become mushy if overcooked, so keep
taking little nibbles while they are blanching.

Drain the parsnips well, then toss them with the
melted butter, parmesan cheese, nutmeg, and a little salt. Chill the mixture until it is firm, about 30
minutes.

When you are ready to serve, form the mixture
into patties, about 2 inches in diameter. Dredge the
patties well in flour, shaking off the excess. Heat the
remaining butter in a large skillet over medium
heat and sauté the patties until crisp and golden, 3
to 4 minutes on each side. Serve hot.

DANDELION FRITTERS

6 to 8 medium-size fritters

7 cups fresh dandelion greens, washed, cooked, and
chopped
2 cloves garlic, crushed
1 medium onion, finely minced
2 eggs, beaten
Salt and pepper
Oat flour, enough to bind mixture into patties

Combine all ingredients in a bowl, mix well, and
form into flat patties. Fry in a small amount of vegetable oil until golden brown. Serve hot.

STEWED SWEET PEPPERS

Serves 4 to 6

There are many variations of this stew, called peperonata and usually served as an appetizer in Italy. Sometimes it is made without any herbs, including garlic, and sometimes basil replaces marjoram or oregano; often it does not have tomato. The dish lends itself to improvisation. Try adding a few tablespoons of dry white wine and stewing it a few minutes longer for another Italian version. It is a versatile late summer dish: colorful, always tasty, easily doubled, and good hot or at room temperature. Like many stews, it tastes even better when made ahead of time. We like to serve it with crusty bread and cheese for lunch.

3 large sweet bell peppers; 1 red, 1 yellow, and 1 green
3 to 4 tablespoons olive oil
1 small onion, sliced lengthwise in 1/4-inch slivers
2 garlic cloves, slivered
1 large tomato, diced, optional
Leaves from 1 or 2 oregano and/or marjoram sprigs
Salt and freshly ground pepper

Wash the peppers, stem and seed them, and remove any large ribs. Cut them lengthwise into 3/8-inch strips.

Heat the olive oil in a skillet. Sauté the peppers over medium heat, stirring occasionally, for about 5 minutes. Add the onion and garlic to the pan and cook for about 5 minutes.

If you are using the tomato, add it to the pan. Cook for about 3 minutes, stirring occasionally.

Add the oregano and/or marjoram and season with salt and pepper. Lower the heat, stir the ingredients, cover the pan, and cook for about 10 minutes or a few minutes longer. Serve hot or at room temperature.

A MESS OF SPRING GREENS

Serves 4 to 6

The greens listed below may be replaced by others, according to availability, and your taste. For example, if you are so fortunate as to have no baby dandelions in your yard, or have no Good-King-Henry in your garden, substitute beet, turnip, or mustard greens. The balance of primary flavors—sour, bitter, salty—is what makes the dish appealing.

2 handfuls small dandelion leaves, about 3 inches long
2 handfuls small sorrel leaves
2 handfuls small Good-King-Henry leaves

1 1/2 pounds spinach
2 tablespoons fruity olive oil
1 tablespoon balsamic vinegar, or to taste
Pinch of salt
Freshly ground pepper
1 small bunch chives, optional

Remove the stems from the spinach and any tough stems from the herbs. Wash the herbs together, and the spinach separately.

Add the dandelion, sorrel, and Good-King-Henry, with the water that clings to their leaves, to a large, noncorrodible pot with a tight-fitting lid. Add the olive oil and stir the greens.

Bring the greens to a simmer over medium heat, then reduce heat to low. Sweat the greens for about 15 minutes, stirring once or twice.

Add the spinach and stir the mixture. Cook over low heat for 10 minutes. Season with balsamic vinegar, salt, and pepper to taste. Serve the greens hot. If desired, snip the chives and toss them with the greens just before serving.

CARROTS WITH HORSERADISH

Serves 4 to 6

This is a fabulous way to prepare carrots; guests are astonished when the secret ingredient is revealed. When cooked, the horseradish turns nutty sweet, and its flavor complements that of the carrots.

1 pound carrots
3 tablespoons unsalted butter
2 tablespoons freshly grated or prepared horseradish, or to taste
1 teaspoon lemon juice
Salt and freshly ground white pepper
2 tablespoons slivered almonds or 1 tablespoon toasted sesame seeds (optional)

Peel the carrots and cut them diagonally into 1/2-inch slices. Steam them for about 5 minutes until they are crisp tender. Remove from heat and drain.

Melt the butter in a sauté pan. Add the horseradish and stir for about 1 minute. Add the drained carrots and sauté them for about 3 minutes. Sprinkle with the lemon juice, and season lightly with salt and freshly ground pepper. Stir for another minute or so and taste for seasoning. Garnish the carrots with the optional almonds or sesame seeds, and serve hot.

Carrots with Horseradish, recipe opposite, and Endive and Raddichio Salad, recipe on page 37.

JAMAICAN-STYLE GREENS

Serves 4 to 6

This method of preparing greens originated in Jamaica, where allspice is used in many ways, from allspice liqueur to elaborate marinades for chicken and goat.

2 pounds spinach, chard, kale, or a combination
2 tablespoons butter
2 tablespoons vegetable oil
1 small onion, diced fine
1/2 teaspoon freshly ground allspice, or to taste
Salt and freshly ground pepper to taste
1 or 2 dashes Angostura bitters
Optional: 1 small chile pepper, minced

Stem and wash the greens and put them in a noncorrodible pot with the water that clings to the leaves. Cook, covered, over medium heat until wilted.

Heat the butter and oil in a skillet over medium heat and sauté the onion for about 5 minutes, stirring occasionally. Roughly chop the wilted greens and add them to the skillet along with allspice, salt and pepper, bitters, and chile as desired. Stir well, cover, and cook over low heat for about 10 minutes. Adjust seasoning if necessary. Serve hot.

NEW POTATOES AND PEAS IN DILL SAUCE

Serves 4 to 6

This dish combines three treats from the garden or farmer's market in a way so satisfying that it can be served as a main course. The peas and potatoes may be cooked ahead and reheated thoroughly in the sauce; undercook them slightly if you do this. Shelling garden peas is soothing work, but edible-pod peas, also called sugar snaps or mangetout peas, taste just as good and cut down the preparation and cooking times.

1 1/2 pounds golf-ball-size new potatoes
1 1/2 pounds fresh garden peas, or 1 pound
*   edible-pod peas*
3 tablespoons butter
2 tablespoons flour
1 1/4 cups milk or half-and-half
Salt and freshly ground pepper to taste
Dash cayenne pepper
1/3 cup chopped dill
2 tablespoons lemon juice, or to taste

Scrub the potatoes well but do not pare them. Halve them and cook in lightly salted boiling water 10 to 15 minutes, or until just tender. Drain and keep warm.

Shell the garden peas or string the edible-pod peas. Place them in a large skillet with water to half-cover them. Cover with a tight-fitting lid and cook 3 to 10 minutes, or until just tender. Drain and keep warm.

Meanwhile, melt the butter in a saucepan and stir in the flour. Cook over low heat, stirring constantly, for 5 minutes. Stir in the milk or half-and-half and cook over low heat for about 10 minutes. Season with salt, pepper, and cayenne. Stir in the dill and lemon juice.

Combine the peas, potatoes, and sauce in a large skillet and heat through over medium heat. Adjust the seasoning and serve hot.

ITALIAN VEGETABLE RAGOUT

Serves 6

This healthful ragout features a variety of vegetables and herbs and is low in fat and cholesterol. It cooks so quickly that it can easily be prepared for a week night meal.

1 pound boiling potatoes, peeled and cut into 1 1/2-inch
*   cubes*
1 pound Brussels sprouts, tough leaves removed, ends
*   trimmed, and cut in half*
1 medium cauliflower, cut into large florets
1 pound Swiss chard, tough stems removed and torn into
*   bite-size pieces*
2 tablespoons olive oil
1 cup chopped onion
1 cup chopped celery
3 large garlic cloves, finely chopped
1 tablespoon fresh marjoram leaves, or 1 teaspoon dried
1 large zucchini, ends trimmed and cut into 1-inch cubes
2 large carrots, peeled and sliced thickly on the diagonal
1 teaspoon coarse salt
1/4 teaspoon freshly ground black pepper
1 16-ounce can chick peas, drained and rinsed with
*   water*
1/4 cup chopped fresh basil, for garnish

Bring a large pot of salted water to a boil. Cook potatoes, Brussels sprouts and cauliflower 5 minutes. Add Swiss chard and boil 1 minute more. Reserve 1/2 cup of the cooking liquid. Drain the vegetables and set aside.

Heat oils in a large Dutch oven over medium-high heat. Add onion, celery, and garlic, and sauté 3 minutes. Stir in marjoram, reserved cooking liquid, tomatoes, zucchini, carrots, salt, pepper, and reserved vegetables. Stir well, cover, and cook over medium-low heat until vegetables are just cooked through, 15 to 20 minutes.

Stir in chick peas and just heat through. Transfer to a serving dish and garnish with chopped basil. Serve over whole wheat spaghetti or steamed brown rice.

THAI-STYLE STIR-FRY

Serves 4

This vegetable stir-fry is fast and easy. Onion and scallions may be used in place of the leeks, and the quantities of the various vegetables may be varied as well. (Don't use more than the first 2 inches of the green, leafy part of the leek; it tends to be stringy.) The perfumy flavor of the feathery cilantro brightens and complements the flavor of both the eggplants and the chiles. Adjust the amount of chile paste or chiles to taste. Serve this dish with brown or white rice and cold beer.

3 tablespoons peanut or vegetable oil
1 large or two medium leeks, rinsed well and cut into 1/4-inch slices
1 large eggplant, peeled and cut into 1/2-inch dice
1 small red or green bell pepper, seeded and cut into strips about 1/4 by 1 inch
2 or 3 large cloves garlic, minced
1/4 pound mushrooms, brushed clean and sliced thinly
3 teaspoons red chile paste or 4 to 6 fresh hot chiles, minced
3 tablespoons water
1 1/2 tablespoons yellow bean paste
4 tablespoons soy sauce
1 1/2 tablespoons rice wine vinegar, or to taste
1 1/2 teaspoons sugar
Salt
3 tablespoons coarsely chopped cilantro
Cilantro sprigs for garnish

Heat the oil in a large skillet or wok over medium heat and sauté the leeks for a minute. Add the eggplant and cook for 3 minutes, stirring well. Add the bell pepper and garlic and stir for a few minutes more. Add the mushrooms, stir, and sauté for about 2 minutes. Cover the pan, reduce heat to medium low, and let cook for a few minutes.

Meanwhile, combine the red chile paste or chiles with the hot water and stir with a fork until the paste is dissolved. Stir in the bean paste, 3 tablespoons soy sauce, vinegar, and sugar. Add this sauce to the pan and toss well to distribute evenly. Cover for a minute or two, then add the cilantro, stir, and cover for 1 minute more.

Taste and add salt, soy sauce, or vinegar if necessary. Spoon over rice, garnish, and serve.

HOT MARINATED MUSHROOMS

Serves 4

2 tablespoons butter
2 tablespoons chopped shallots
1/2 pound fresh mushrooms, cleaned and sliced
1 tablespoon lemon juice
2 tablespoons white wine
1 tablespoon water
1/4 cup freshly chopped parsley
1/2 teaspoon fresh tarragon
1/4 teaspoon hot pepper sauce
Freshly ground black pepper
4 thick slices homemade whole wheat bread, warmed

Melt butter in a heavy skillet on medium-high heat and sauté onions. Add mushrooms and reduce heat slightly. Sauté about 1 minute. Add lemon juice, wine, water, herbs, hot pepper sauce, and black pepper to taste. Increase the heat to high and simmer until the juices are slightly reduced. Do not overcook the mushrooms. To serve, spoon one-quarter of the mushrooms onto each slice of bread and drizzle juices over top. Can also be served as a hot relish with steak, chicken, or omelet.

Poultry, meat & seafood

BRAISED CHICKEN WITH MACE AND TOMATOES

Serves 6

In this dish, the acidity of the tomatoes and wine plays off the mace and a touch of sugar to create a subtle sweet/sour flavor. If you can't find bucatini, use spaghetti.

1 3- to 3 1/2-pound chicken
Salt and freshly ground black pepper to taste
3 tablespoons olive oil
1 medium onion, diced fine
2 garlic cloves, minced
1 pound tomatoes, fresh or canned, peeled, seeded if
  desired, and diced
1 bay leaf
1 1/2 teaspoons mace blades or 2 teaspoons ground mace
1 cup dry white wine
Pinch of sugar
1 pound hollow pasta, such as bucatini or perciatelli
Garnishes: Coarsely chopped leaves from 4 or 5 sprigs of
  Italian parsley; about 1/2 cup freshly grated Italian
  parmesan or romano cheese

Cut chicken into serving pieces, rinse, and pat dry. Season lightly with salt and pepper. Heat oil over medium high heat in large skillet. Brown chicken on all sides, about 15 minutes.

Remove chicken to plate and remove excess fat from pan, leaving about 2 tablespoons. Add onions and garlic and cook over low heat, covered, until the vegetables are softened, about 10 minutes.

Add tomatoes, bay leaf, mace, wine, and sugar and bring sauce to a simmer for 15 minutes. Add chicken and cook over medium low heat, covered, for 30 minutes, until chicken is done. Turn the chicken occasionally. Alternatively, you may braise the browned chicken in a 325° F oven for 45 minutes to an hour.

Cook the pasta *al dente* in a large quantity of boiling salted water. Adjust the seasoning of the sauce. Toss the drained pasta with the sauce and place on a heated platter. Place chicken pieces on top and serve. Garnish with chopped parsley and grated cheese.

Chicken Saté (or Satay) with Peanut Sauce

Serves 6 to 8

Soaking the bamboo skewers overnight helps keep their tips from burning. The saté has the best flavor if the meat is grilled, but it may be cooked under a broiler. Pork is often used for satés, and medium-sized shrimp produce very tasty results.

Chicken and Marinade

20 6-inch bamboo skewers
1 heaping tablespoon tamarind paste
2 whole chicken breasts, about 2 pounds with bone in
2 tablespoons Thai or Vietnamese fish sauce
1 tablespoon brown sugar
1 tablespoon vegetable oil
1 garlic clove, peeled
1 tablespoon chopped cilantro roots or 2 tablespoons chopped stems

Soak the skewers in water all day or overnight, turning them occasionally. Dissolve the tamarind paste in 1/4 cup boiling water. Strain the paste, pressing on the solids, and discard the seeds and pulp.

Bone and skin the chicken breasts and separate the fillets. Remove the tendon from each half breast. Slice the pieces separately on a very sharp diagonal about 1/4 inch thick.

Mix the fish sauce, dissolved tamarind paste, brown sugar, and vegetable oil together in a shallow dish large enough to hold the chicken. Crush the garlic and cilantro roots or stems together in a mortar and pestle, or pulverize them in a spice grinder. Mix the herbs with the other marinade ingredients.

Toss the chicken in the marinade, coating the pieces evenly. Marinate the chicken for an hour or so at cool room temperature.

Thread the chicken on the skewers and prepare a fire or preheat the broiler.

Sauce

2 garlic cloves, minced
1 shallot, diced
2 teaspoons vegetable oil
1/2 tablespoon tamarind paste
1 stalk (6 to 8 inches long) fresh lemongrass, minced, or 2 teaspoons lemongrass powder or 3 stalks dried lemongrass, soaked in hot water, then minced
1 tablespoon brown sugar
1 teaspoon dark soy sauce, or to taste
1/8 teaspoon red pepper flakes, or to taste
3 tablespoons peanut butter
1 cup water

Soften the garlic and shallot in the vegetable oil over low heat. Dissolve the tamarind paste in 3 tablespoons boiling water. Strain the paste and discard the seeds and pulp. Add the strained tamarind to the pan with the garlic and shallots. Stir in the lemongrass, sugar, soy sauce, red pepper flakes, and peanut butter. Gradually stir in the water.

Cook over low heat for 5 minutes. Keep the sauce just below the simmering point, or it will thicken too much. To thin it or to reheat it, stir in a tablespoon or so of water.

Grill or broil the chicken until it is just done, about 2 minutes on each side. Serve the chicken very hot with the sauce in separate dishes.

Roasted Chicken Breasts with Herb Leaves

Serves 6

In this elegant recipe, the skin is left on the chicken breasts, and the herb leaves are placed under the skin for maximum flavor.

6 boneless chicken breast halves, skin on
1½ cups wild rice
12 oregano leaves
12 small basil leaves
12 sage leaves
12 thin slices fresh ginger (the size of a dime)
3 garlic cloves, each cut into 4 slices

Sauce

1 teaspoon chopped oregano
1 teaspoon chopped basil
1 teaspoon chopped sage
1/2 teaspoon minced fresh ginger
1 clove garlic, minced
1 tablespoon soy sauce
1 tablespoon melted butter
1 teaspoon Dijon-style mustard
1½ tablespoons butter

Begin cooking wild rice in water for 45–60 minutes or according to package directions. Carefully lift the skin of each chicken breast half away from the meat, and place two each of oregano, basil, and sage leaves and slices of ginger and garlic under the skin.

Combine all sauce ingredients and heat. Bake chicken for 30 minutes at 375° F, basting with sauce two or three times during cooking. Toss the wild rice with butter and serve with chicken.

Frango Guisado a Mode de Maria Gloria (Chicken to the Glory of Mary), recipe opposite.
Golden Saffron Rice recipe on page 43.

FRANGO GUISADO A MODA DE MARIA GLORIA

Serves 10 to 12

2 frying chickens, cut into serving pieces
Butter, margarine, or olive oil as needed
3 to 4 tablespoons flour
6 cloves garlic, peeled
1 teaspoon each ground coriander, cumin, and fennel seed
1/2 teaspoon ground caraway seed
2 cups dry white wine
3 to 4 bay leaves, fresh or dried
1 cup chicken broth
2 cups heavy cream
Salt and pepper to taste
Chopped fresh parsley to garnish

In a heavy large skillet or Dutch oven, sauté chicken pieces in butter or oil, adding butter or oil as needed. Sprinkle flour over chicken and blend into pan juices.

While chicken is browning, place garlic, ground seeds, and about 1/2 cup wine in blender. Blend until smooth. Pour over chicken and add remaining wine and broth. Mix well; cover and cook over low heat until meat is tender. Remove chicken to serving dish. Stir cream into remaining juices, and cook over medium heat 5 to 10 minutes until thickened. Pour over chicken and garnish with chopped parsley.

MARJORAM GRILLED CHICKEN BREASTS WITH DILL-CHIVE SAUCE

Serves 6

The marjoram–olive oil marinade gives the chicken breast a colorful, crusty coating to which the creamy dill-chive sauce adds a refreshing touch.

6 boneless, skinless chicken breast halves
2 tablespoons olive oil
1 tablespoon fresh lemon juice
6 tablespoons fresh marjoram
1/2 teaspoon freshly ground pepper
3/4 cup sour cream
3/4 cup nonfat yogurt
1/2 teaspoon salt
1/4 teaspoon white pepper
2 tablespoons fresh dill weed
1/4 cup fresh chives

Pound chicken pieces to a uniform thickness so that they will cook evenly. Rub them with olive oil and lemon juice, and sprinkle with marjoram and pepper. Marinate them in the refrigerator for at least one hour. Heat a griddle or large frying pan to medium-high. Add chicken, cook 2 minutes, and turn. Cook 4 to 8 minutes longer or until cooked through. Combine sour cream, yogurt, salt, pepper, dill, and chives, and serve this sauce either over the chicken or as a condiment.

GARLIC ORANGE CHICKEN

Serves 6

In this recipe, the celerylike flavor of lovage associates wonderfully with basil and chives, as does the chicken with the vermicelli pasta.

6 boneless, skinless chicken breast halves
6 cloves garlic, peeled and halved
1½ tablespoons oil
1½ cups chopped onion
1/4 teaspoon pepper
1/2 teaspoon salt
1/2 teaspoon dry mustard
1 cup orange juice
1 cup chicken broth
1/4 cup chopped fresh basil
1/4 cup chopped chives
3 tablespoons chopped lovage
12 ounces vermicelli
1½ tablespoons cornstarch mixed with
  2 tablespoons water
6 sprigs basil and 6 chive (or other herb) flowers
  for garnish

Trim any fat from the chicken. Open two small pockets in each breast half, either by slicing into it with a knife or by separating the muscles of the breast. Insert a piece of garlic in each pocket. Pat the chicken dry. In a heavy skillet, brown the chicken on both sides in the oil, then remove it. Add onion to skillet, reduce heat and cook until softened and lightly browned, about 3 minutes. Add the pepper, salt, and mustard, and cook for 1 minute, stirring the browned onion bits into mixture. Add orange juice, broth, and herbs. Bring mixture to a boil, add chicken, then cover and simmer for 20 minutes. Cook vermicelli while chicken is simmering. Remove chicken from pan and keep warm. Bring the sauce to a boil. Add cornstarch-water mixture and stir constantly until thickened. Spoon some of the sauce over the chicken and the remainder over the hot vermicelli. Garnish with the basil sprigs and chive flowers.

DILLED CHICKEN POT PIE

Serves 4 to 6

This is a perfect way to use leftover roasted or poached chicken and vegetables, or you may make it from scratch. Turkey substitutes nicely for the chicken. Try this dish with different vegetables: artichoke hearts or asparagus make a deluxe filling, and mushrooms are a good addition.

Filling

3 tablespoons butter
1/2 cup finely diced celery
1/2 cup finely diced onion
1 small bay leaf
3 tablespoons flour
1^1/$_2$ cups chicken stock
1^1/$_2$ cups milk or cream
Dash or two of Tabasco sauce
Salt and freshly ground black pepper to taste
1^1/$_2$ to 2 cups shredded or diced cooked chicken meat
3/4 pound diced cooked potatoes
1/2 pound diced cooked carrots
4 to 6 ounces cooked green peas, or use green beans cut in 1-inch pieces
1/2 cup chopped dill

Melt the butter over low heat in a large saucepan. Add the celery, onion, and bay leaf, cover, and cook about 10 minutes, or until the vegetables are soft.

Sprinkle the flour over the vegetables, stir well to incorporate, then cook for about 5 minutes.

Stir in the chicken stock and the milk or cream. Cook the sauce over low heat for 15 minutes, stirring occasionally. Remove the bay leaf and add the Tabasco, salt, and pepper.

Stir in the chicken, potatoes, carrots, peas or beans, and dill. Keep the filling warm while you make the biscuit dough.

Biscuits

1 cup sifted all-purpose flour
1^1/$_2$ teaspoons baking powder
1/4 teaspoon salt
3 tablespoons cold butter or vegetable shortening, or a combination
1/2 cup milk
3 tablespoons chopped dill

Preheat the oven to 425° F.

Sift the flour, baking powder, and salt together into a bowl. Make a well in the mixture and cut the fat into the dry ingredients. Add the milk and dill and stir the mixture with a fork for about a minute, or until the dough leaves the sides of the bowl.

Transfer the chicken and vegetable mixture to a 3-quart ovenproof casserole. Drop the dough over the filling with a large spoon, spacing it evenly, to make six biscuits.

Bake for 20 to 25 minutes, or until the biscuits are lightly browned and the pie is bubbling. Serve hot.

CHICKEN BREASTS WITH HERBS IN PARCHMENT

Serves 6

Lemon thyme and marjoram give this recipe a delightfully different taste.

6 boneless, skinless chicken breast halves
4 cups chicken or vegetable broth
3/4 cup julienned carrots
3/4 cup peeled and julienned broccoli stems
5 teaspoons butter
2 tablespoons flour
1/2 teaspoon salt
1/4 teaspoon white pepper
1/16 teaspoon cayenne pepper
1/3 cup sliced scallions
1/2 cup whole milk
1/2 cup chicken broth
2 tablespoons white wine
2 tablespoons lemon thyme leaves
3 tablespoons chopped parsley
1 tablespoon chopped marjoram
1^1/$_2$ pounds small new potatoes

Poach chicken breasts by placing in broth and bringing to a boil. Cover pan and remove from heat. Let chicken remain in broth (without uncovering) for 15 minutes, then remove. Steam carrots and broccoli for about 3 minutes, just until tender, and set aside. Melt butter, add flour, salt, pepper, and cayenne, and cook until smooth and golden, stirring constantly. Add scallions and cook 2 more minutes. Stir in milk and broth and continue stirring until sauce thickens. Add wine and herbs and stir to combine. Place a chicken breast on each of six 10-by-12-inch pieces of foil or oiled cooking parchment. Cover each piece of chicken with 1/6 of the vegetables and 1/6 of the sauce. Bring ends together and crimp or fold, then bring sides together and crimp or fold, making an airtight package for each piece of chicken. Bake for 20 minutes at 350° F. Steam potatoes while chicken is baking. Carefully open and fold back foil or paper, and place a serving of potatoes around the chicken in each packet.

POULTRY, MEAT, AND SEAFOOD

Dilled Chicken Pot Pie, recipe opposite.

ISLAND ROASTED CHICKEN WITH THYME MUSTARD SAUCE

Serves 3 to 4

In this dish, the cavity of the chicken is stuffed with garlic, whole stems of thyme, and spices of the islands. The entrée is accompanied by a sharp mustard sauce redolent of thyme.

Seasoning mixture

1/2 teaspoon ground allspice
1/2 teaspoon ground nutmeg
1/2 teaspoon ground clove
1/2 teaspoon ground cinnamon
1/2 teaspoon ground cayenne pepper
1/4 teaspoon salt
1 tablespoon butter, softened
1 whole chicken (3 to 4 pounds), washed
6 to 8 garlic cloves, slivered
1/2 tablespoon whole cloves
10 to 12 stems fresh common thyme, 4 to 6 inches long
1 cup Thyme Mustard Sauce (see below), warmed

Preheat oven to 375° F. Combine the seasoning mixture in a small bowl. Spread the butter evenly over the chicken and in the cavity. Insert the garlic and cloves under the skin over the breasts and legs and also inside the cavity. Sprinkle the seasoning mixture over the entire chicken and put some under the skin and inside the cavity. Stuff the thyme stems under the skin and in the cavity.

Place the chicken in a roasting pan and roast for about an hour and 15 minutes, or until a leg can be twisted easily. Baste every 15 minutes with the pan juices.

Remove the chicken from the pan and place it on a serving platter. Garnish with the thyme stems and garlic, forming a crown around the chicken. Pass the Thyme Mustard Sauce at the table.

Thyme Mustard Sauce—*Makes 1 cup*

3/4 cup light or heavy cream
1/4 cup Dijon-style mustard
3 tablespoons fresh thyme leaves
1/8 teaspoon white pepper

Combine all ingredients in a small bowl. At serving time, warm the mustard sauce in a microwave until it simmers, or place it on top of a double boiler and bring it to the desired temperature. Serve at the table with Island Roasted Chicken. This sauce also makes a nice condiment for steak au poivre, roast pork or lamb, or broiled fish.

BRAISED CHICKEN WITH CREAMY HERB SAUCE

Serves 6

Chervil, sage, and lemon verbena lend this recipe a surprisingly subtle flavor.

6 boneless, skinless chicken breast halves
2 tablespoons butter
1 tablespoon oil
1 1/2 cups sliced red onions
1 cup coarsely sliced carrots
2 tablespoons chopped chervil
2 tablespoons chopped lemon verbena
3 tablespoons chopped sage leaves
2/3 cup chicken broth
2 tablespoons white wine
1/4 teaspoon salt
1/4 teaspoon white pepper
2 tablespoons whole milk
2 tablespoons fresh lemon juice
Additional chervil for garnish
1 16-ounce loaf French bread

Heat butter and oil and brown chicken breasts, then lift chicken out and set aside. Add onions and carrots to pan and stir to coat with oil. Add herbs, broth, and wine. Lay chicken on top of vegetable mixture and sprinkle with salt and pepper. Cover and simmer 20 minutes. Remove chicken from pan and keep warm. In a blender or food processor, puree cooking liquid and vegetables. Add milk and blend, then add lemon juice and blend. Pour sauce over chicken, reheating if necessary, and garnish with the additional chervil leaves. Serve with warm, sliced French bread.

CHICKEN ROSEMARY

Serves 6

8 boneless, skinned chicken breast halves
leaves from 4 sprigs of fresh rosemary, or use 3 table-
* spoons dried rosemary*
5 tablespoons apricot preserves
5 tablespoons butter or margarine, softened
1 large clove garlic, minced

Preheat oven to 350° F. Flatten chicken breast halves slightly. Mix together rosemary, apricot preserves, butter, and garlic. Spread 1 tablespoon of this mixture on each breast, roll up, and secure with a skewer or tie with string. Place rolls in ovenproof casserole, and spread remaining rosemary mixture on top. Cover and bake for 45 minutes, or until done.

Remove chicken to a warmed platter. Reduce the pan juices until thick, and pour over the chicken.

HERBED CHICKEN BREASTS CARIBBEAN

Serves 6

3 tablespoons brown sugar
1/2 teaspoon nutmeg
1/4 teaspoon cinnamon
1/4 teaspoon white pepper
1/4 teaspoon allspice
1/3 cup fresh lime juice
6 boneless, skinless chicken breast halves
1 tablespoon oil
2 cups raw white rice, cooked according to
*   package instructions*
2 tablespoons broth
2 tablespoons dry sherry
2 tablespoons white wine
2 tablespoons butter
1/4 cup chopped marjoram
2 tablespoons chopped rosemary
2 tablespoons chopped sage

In a small bowl, combine the first six ingredients. Heat oil in a skillet, and brown chicken for 1 minute on each side. Reduce heat and continue to sauté chicken for 10 minutes, turning once. Begin cooking rice according to package instructions while chicken is cooking. Transfer chicken to a platter and keep warm. Add 2 tablespoons broth to skillet and stir it around to loosen the browned bits. Add the brown sugar mixture and cook for 2 minutes or until thickened a bit. Add sherry and white wine and bring to a boil. Reduce heat and whisk in butter, 1 tablespoon at a time, incorporating the first tablespoon before adding the next. Return chicken to pan, place herbs on top of it, and add any juices that accumulated on the platter. Baste with sauce in pan (carefully, so as not to dislodge herbs from chicken), and cook over medium heat for 10 minutes or until done. Serve with rice.

Meat

LAMB ROAST WITH HERBES DE PROVENCE CRUST

Serves 6

The herbal crust on this savory roast enhances both the succulent lamb and the steamed winter vegetables that accompany it. The crust would complement pork as well.

6 tablespoons Dijon-style mustard
1¹/₂ tablespoons soy sauce
2 large garlic cloves, minced
1¹/₂ tablespoons herbes de Provence
1¹/₂ tablespoons olive oil
2-pound boneless lamb roast, trimmed of excess fat
*   and tied*

Place the mustard, soy, garlic, and herbs in a blender or food processor. With the machine running, gradually add the oil. Coat the entire surface of the roast with the mustard mixture. Cover carefully and refrigerate for several hours or overnight.

Place the lamb on a rack set on a tray in an oven preheated to 400° F. Immediately turn the heat down to 350° and roast 1 hour (for medium rare) to 1 hour and 15 minutes (for medium). If using a meat thermometer, roast until it reads 140° for medium rare or 150° for medium. Do not overcook. Allow the lamb to rest 15 minutes on a heated platter before carving.

YELLOW BEEF CURRY

Serves 6 to 8

Thai and Cambodian curries are quite thin, almost soupy, to flavor the large quantities of rice served with them. This versatile yellow curry paste can also be used with steamed or poached chicken or duck. Remove cooked meat from the bones and simmer it in the curry for about 10 minutes, or chop the poultry into pieces with a cleaver, leaving the skin on and simmer the pieces for 15 to 20 minutes, until they are tender and done.

Yellow Curry Paste—*Makes about 1 cup*

This recipe makes enough for three to five dishes of curry, each serving six to eight people. The paste will keep its flavor for several months if frozen. It also keeps for about a month if refrigerated in a tightly closed container with a film of oil on top of the paste.

6 small dried red chiles, such as serranos or cayennes
3 shallots, chopped
4 large garlic cloves, chopped
2 stalks (6 to 8 inches long) fresh lemongrass, chopped,
  or 4 teaspoons lemongrass powder or 6 stalks dried
  lemongrass, soaked in hot water, then chopped
1 tablespoon chopped fresh cilantro root or
  2 tablespoons chopped fresh stems
1 2-inch piece of greater galangal root, peeled and
  chopped, or 1 teaspoon galangal powder
2 fresh red serrano chiles, seeded and chopped, or
  a 1-inch-wide piece of sweet red pepper
1 2-inch piece turmeric root, peeled and chopped, or
  1 tablespoon turmeric powder
1 tablespoon freshly toasted and ground coriander seed
1 teaspoon freshly toasted and ground cumin seed
1 teaspoon white peppercorns, ground in a spice grinder
  or mortar and pestle
1 teaspoon dried shrimp paste, or 1/2 teaspoon
  anchovy paste
1 teaspoon salt
2 tablespoons vegetable oil
Optional: 3 pieces Kaffir lime rind, soaked in hot water
  and chopped, or 1/2 teaspoon powdered Kaffir lime

Seed the dried chiles and soak them in 2 tablespoons boiling water for about 10 minutes.

Place all ingredients in a blender jar and blend to a paste, stopping to scrape down the jar and redistribute the ingredients to ensure a smooth paste. Add more water, a tablespoon at a time, if necessary.

Beef Curry

2 pounds round steak
1 14-ounce can unsweetened coconut milk
3 tablespoons yellow curry paste (see recipe above)
1 tablespoon Thai or Vietnamese fish sauce, or to taste
10 to 12 holy basil leaves or medium-sized
  sweet basil leaves
Salt to taste

Trim the steak of fat and connective tissue and cut it into 1/4-inch-thick slices about 1/2 inch wide and 2 inches long.

Stir the canned coconut milk very well. Add half of it to a wok. This is the "thick" coconut milk that will be used to fry the curry paste. Stir 1 cup of water into the remaining coconut milk to make "thin" coconut milk.

Simmer the thick coconut milk over low heat until it is reduced slightly and some oil begins to appear, about 5 minutes. Stir in the curry paste and cook about 5 minutes longer, stirring occasionally. The paste will smell cooked, and oil will begin to rise when the curry and coconut have cooked long enough.

Add the sliced beef and stir well. Add the thin coconut milk and the fish sauce and bring the curry to a boil. Reduce heat and simmer until the beef is tender, about 15 minutes. Add more water if the curry thickens. Season the curry with salt to taste. Stir in the basil leaves 2 or 3 minutes before the curry is done. Serve hot with plenty of rice, preferably basmati.

HUNGARIAN SZEGED GOULASH

Yield: 6 generous servings

Szeged, a city in southern Hungary, is famous for its paprika, which, along with sage and caraway, figures prominently in our version of this classic dish. Dumplings are a traditional and delicious accompaniment.

4 ounces lean bacon, cut into 1/2-inch pieces
2 pounds boneless pork, trimmed of fat and cut
  into 1-inch cubes
1 large red onion, chopped coarsely
2 large cloves garlic, minced
2 tablespoons flour
2 tablespoons sweet Hungarian paprika
2 teaspoons caraway seed
1 tablespoon chopped fresh sage
2 teaspoons chopped fresh rosemary
1 tablespoon chopped fresh sweet marjoram or
  mild oregano
2 teaspoons chopped fresh thyme
1 teaspoon salt
1/2 teaspoon freshly ground black pepper
2 cups apple juice or cider, or use frozen apple juice
  diluted with 2 parts water instead of 3
2 pounds sauerkraut, drained and rinsed
2–3 tart apples, cored and sliced
1 cup sour cream
Steamed diced or sliced red potatoes, spaetzle, or
  egg noodles tossed in a small amount of
  melted butter to moisten
Chopped fresh dill and parsley for garnish

In a large, deep roasting pan or Dutch oven, sauté bacon until crisp. Remove with a slotted spoon and set aside, leaving 1 to 2 tablespoons of fat in the pan. Add pork cubes gradually, stirring to brown on all sides. Stir in onion and garlic, and cook until onion softens.

Sprinkle flour, paprika, and seasonings over vegetables and meat and stir to combine, letting mixture brown slightly. Add apple juice and sauerkraut; mix well. Reduce heat, cover, and cook about 45 minutes, or until meat is tender. Stir occasionally and add additional apple juice or water if needed.

During the last 10 minutes of cooking, stir in apples and simmer, covered, until apples are just tender. Do not overcook. Dish can easily be prepared ahead up to this point and then reheated.

When ready to serve, stir in sour cream, adding a small amount of liquid if meat mixture is too dry. There should be plenty of sauce. Heat through but do not boil. Serve with steamed red potatoes, spaetzle, or noodles. Garnish with dill, parsley, and reserved bacon, broken into pieces.

CAMBODIAN CREPES

Serves 4 to 8

Many cooks make the crepes with eggs, though they can be made with a rice flour and coconut milk batter which cooks slowly in a special wok. As part of a Cambodian dinner, bring the crepes to the table and cut them in half to serve; they are not as elegant as when they are served whole, but no one complains because they are so delicious. Serve individual crepes before simple dinners, usually grilled fish or chicken marinated in Thai fish sauce, garlic, and cilantro. A complementary salad to serve with such a dinner consists of strips of fresh cabbage, tender cilantro leaves and stems, and julienne carrot and cucumber arranged attractively on a platter, dressed with Cambodian hot sauce.

Batter

2 extra large eggs
1/3 cup all-purpose flour
1/3 cup water
1/4 teaspoon salt
1/4 teaspoon powdered turmeric

Whisk the eggs well. Gradually whisk in the flour, then the water. Add the salt and turmeric and whisk well. Cover the batter and let stand at room temperature an hour or two. Store in the refrigerator as long as 8 hours, bringing to room temperature before cooking the crepes.

Cook the crepes in a lightly oiled 8- or 9-inch skillet which has been heated thoroughly over medium-high heat.

Add 1/4 cup batter to the skillet and swirl the pan to cover it evenly with the batter. Cook, for 45 to 60 seconds, until well browned, then flip crepe and cook other side for 15 to 25 seconds. Stack the crepes on a plate as they are done and keep them warm if you're going to use them right away.

You may cook the crepes ahead, cool them to room temperature, then store them, covered, in the refrigerator for a day. Bring them to room temperature before using them.

Preheat the oven to 500° F.

Filling

2 teaspoons cooking oil
1/3 pound ground pork
1 garlic clove, minced
1/4 cup diced onion
1 teaspoon Thai or Vietnamese fish sauce
1 cup grated carrot
1 cup shredded cabbage
1/4 pound cooked bay shrimp
1/3 pound bean sprouts, about 1 1/2 cups
Several fresh holy or sweet basil leaves, shredded
Several fresh spearmint leaves, shredded
Soy sauce to taste
Garnishes: Cambodian hot sauce, 2 tablespoons
    dry-roasted peanuts, chopped fine

Heat the oil over medium heat and sauté the pork with the garlic and onion until the pork is done. Season the mixture with the fish sauce. Remove extra fat from the pan.

Add the carrot and cabbage and stir-fry the mixture for 1 minute. Remove from heat and stir in the bay shrimp, bean sprouts, basil, and mint. Season with soy or fish sauce.

To finish the crepes, lightly oil a baking sheet. Arrange the crepes on it, shiny side down. Divide the filling among the crepes, and fold them over it. Bake for 5 minutes in the preheated oven. Serve hot with Cambodian hot sauce and chopped peanuts on the side.

VEAL MUSHROOM RAGOUT

Serves 6

This rich veal ragout features rosemary two ways—half is cooked with the ragout, giving a subtle background flavor, while the rest is added after cooking for a fresh rosemary "zing".

$3^{1}/_{2}$ pounds well trimmed veal rump or shoulder,
    cut into $1^{1}/_{2}$-inch cubes
2 tablespoons vegetable oil
2 tablespoons unsalted butter
1 tablespoon unbleached all-purpose flour
1/4 cup finely chopped shallots (about 6 large)
$1^{1}/_{2}$ teaspoons coarse salt
1/4 teaspoon freshly ground black pepper
1 cup chicken broth
1/2 cup dry white wine
$1^{1}/_{2}$ pounds mushrooms, wiped clean,
    ends trimmed and cut in half
1/4 cup chopped fresh rosemary

Preheat the oven to 375° F.

Pat veal cubes dry with paper towel. Heat oil and butter in a large Dutch oven over medium heat. Brown veal well on all sides in 4 or 5 batches without crowding. Add more oil to the pan if necessary. As veal cooks, remove to a plate.

Remove all but 1 tablespoon fat from the pan and return veal to the pan. Add flour, shallots, salt, and pepper and toss well 1 minute. Add the broth, wine, mushrooms and half the rosemary, and bring to a boil. Cover and cook in the preheated oven, stirring once or twice until veal is very tender, about $1^{1}/_{2}$ hours. After cooking, stir in remaining rosemary. Transfer to a serving dish and garnish with parsley. Serve over cooked wide egg noodles.

OXTAIL RAGOUT

Serves 6

You could make this ragout with any stewing cut of beef, but you would then miss the special succulence and glutinous quality of the lowly

3 pounds oxtails, cut into $1^{1}/_{2}$-inch thick pieces
3 tablespoons vegetable oil
2 large garlic cloves, peeled and finely chopped
3 medium leeks, white part only, thinly sliced
3 medium celery ribs, chopped
1 large carrot, peeled and chopped
1 tablespoon unbleached all-purpose flour
$1^{1}/_{2}$ teaspoons coarse salt
1/4 teaspoon freshly ground black pepper

1 tablespoon fresh thyme leaves, or 1 teaspoon dried
1 teaspoon ground mustard
1 cup canned Italian plum tomatoes,
    drained and chopped
1/2 cup dry red wine
1 cup beef broth
1/4 cup chopped Italian parsley, for garnish

Preheat the oven to 350° F.

Pat oxtails dry with paper towels. Heat oil in a large Dutch oven over medium heat. Brown oxtails on all sides in 3 or 4 batches. Add more oil to the pan if necessary. Transfer oxtails to a plate.

Remove all but 1 tablespoon oil from the pan. Add garlic, leek, celery and carrot and stir well, about 1 minute, scraping up any browned bits. Stir in flour, salt and pepper, thyme and mustard and cook 1 minute more. Stir in tomatoes, wine and broth and bring to a boil. Return oxtails to pan and stir well. Cover and cook in the preheated oven until oxtails are very tender, about 3 hours.

Transfer ragout to a serving dish and garnish with chopped parsley. Serve with steamed new potatoes.

CURRIED ORANGE PORK RAGOUT WITH BROCCOLI

Serves 6

$3^{1}/_{2}$ pounds well-trimmed pork butt or shoulder,
    cut into $1^{1}/_{2}$-inch cubes
2 tablespoons vegetable oil
1 tablespoon unsalted butter
1 cup thinly sliced scallions (green and white part)
6 large garlic cloves, finely chopped
1 tablespoon grated fresh ginger
1/4 teaspoon crushed red pepper flakes
2 tablespoons curry powder
1/2 teaspoon ground coriander
1/4 teaspoon ground cumin seed
1 tablespoon unbleached all-purpose flour
1 teaspoon coarse salt
1/4 teaspoon freshly ground black pepper
1 large whole cinnamon stick
zest (colored part of peel) of 2 large navel oranges
1 cup chicken broth
2 tablespoons honey
2 tablespoons dry sherry
2 tablespoons soy sauce
1 large bunch of broccoli (2 pounds)
1/4 cup chopped fresh cilantro for garnish
orange slices, for garnish

From top: Veal Mushroom Ragout, Curried Orange Pork Ragout, and Oxtail Ragout, recipes opposite.

Preheat the oven to 375° F.

Pat pork cubes dry with paper towels. Heat oil and butter in a large Dutch oven over medium heat. Cook pork in 4 or 5 batches without crowding until well browned on all sides. Add more oil to the pan if necessary. Transfer cooked meat to a plate.

Remove all but 1 tablespoon fat from the pan and add the scallions, garlic, and ginger, and cook until wilted, 2 to 3 minutes. Add the red pepper flakes, curry powder, coriander, cumin, flour, salt, and pepper, and cook 2 minutes. Add remaining ingredients except broccoli and bring to a boil. Stir in the reserved pork and cover and cook in the preheated oven until pork is very tender, 1½ hours, stirring once or twice.

While pork is cooking trim broccoli into florets. Reserve stems for another use. Steam broccoli over boiling water until just tender. Stir broccoli into the finished pork ragout. Transfer to a serving dish and garnish with cilantro. Serve over steamed brown or white rice.

NEW YORK STRIP STEAK WITH THYME AND ROSEMARY SALSA

Serves 2

This is a favorite dish. The salsa is an herbal twist on the traditional Mexican condiment and exudes a piquant, camping-outdoors-by-the-fire bouquet. Rosemary's piny essence complements the delectable combination of tomatoes, shallots, jalapeño peppers, and thyme.

1 medium tomato, diced
1/4 cup diced red onion
2 shallot cloves, minced
1 to 2 jalapeño peppers, seeded and minced
1 tablespoon fresh thyme, minced
1 tablespoon fresh rosemary, minced
1/8 teaspoon salt
1 tablespoon butter, melted
2 eight-ounce New York strip steaks, well trimmed
2½ tablespoons dry red wine
2½ tablespoons red wine vinegar
1 teaspoon red hot sauce

Combine the first seven ingredients in a small bowl and set aside. Place the butter and steaks in a heated skillet and cook over medium heat, turning after 5 to 7 minutes. Continue cooking until steaks reach the desired degree of doneness. Remove them to warm serving plates, saving the pan juices in the skillet.

Add to the juices the tomato mixture, red wine, vinegar, and red hot sauce and sauté over moderately high heat for 3 to 5 minutes, or until the tomato and onion are soft. Remove from heat and spoon the salsa over the steaks. Serve immediately, accompanied by a chilled beverage; we suggest a cold beer.

Seafood

TUNISIAN-STYLE SNAPPER

Serves 6

Any white-fleshed, firm fish with large flakes may be used: red snapper, Pacific snapper, rockfish, sea bass, and any kind of cod are all good. Couscous or rice flavored with mint or parsley (or both) will complement the fish well. Harissa is a paste of chile peppers and spices used in North Africa; you can find it at some cookware stores, gourmet shops, or ethnic specialty shops.

1 tablespoon toasted and ground cumin
2 garlic cloves, crushed
2 tablespoons olive oil
Optional: hot red pepper flakes or harissa to taste
2 pounds fish fillets
Salt
Freshly ground black pepper if red pepper is not used
Pure olive oil to fill a sauté pan 1/2 inch deep
About 1 cup flour
1 large lime or 1 medium lemon
Optional garnish: lime or lemon slices

Mix the cumin and crushed garlic with 2 tablespoons olive oil to make a paste, and stir in the optional hot red pepper or harissa. Rub the paste all over the fish fillets, then cover and refrigerate for an hour or two.

When ready to serve, sprinkle fish lightly with salt, and black pepper if desired. Heat olive oil over medium heat in a skillet large enough to cook the fish without crowding.

Dredge fish well in flour, patting to remove excess. When oil shimmers in the pan, add fish fillets. Cook until golden brown on both sides, about 3 to 5 minutes per side, depending on the thickness of the fish. Drain briefly on paper towels, then transfer to a serving platter and squeeze the lime or lemon juice all over the fish. Garnish with optional lime or lemon slices. Serve hot.

PINEAPPLE AND THYME GRILLED ORANGE ROUGHY

Serves 4

This light entrée is ideal for an early summer picnic. The marinade is quick and easy to prepare and can also be used for other firm, mild-flavored fish such as swordfish, halibut, and mahi-mahi.

1 cup pineapple juice
1 cup dry white wine
1/4 cup vegetable oil
1 small red onion, slivered
1 to 2 jalapeño peppers, seeded and minced
1/4 cup fresh lemon thyme or common thyme
1 tablespoon ground cumin
4 eight-ounce orange roughy fillets
1 teaspoon paprika

Combine the first seven ingredients in a shallow dish. Place the fillets in the dish, and marinate and chill for 4 to 6 hours, turning the fillets over at least once.

Preheat the grill until the coals are gray to white. Remove the fillets from the marinade. Lightly oil the grill, place the fish on it, and sprinkle on half the paprika. Turn the fish after 5 to 7 minutes and sprinkle on the remaining paprika. Continue grilling for 5 to 7 minutes more, or until the fish is opaque in the center. Remove to warm plates and serve immediately.

SCALLOPS AND PRAWNS GRILLED ON A BED OF CINNAMON BASIL

Serves 8

1 pound scallops, about 32 medium
2 pounds red or new potatoes, enough to make 32 medium chunks
1/2 pound onions, enough to make 64 pieces
1 pound mushrooms, about 32 medium
1 pound prawns, about 32 medium
1 1/2 tablespoons chicken broth
1/2 tablespoon olive oil
1 pound cinnamon basil

Cut potatoes into 32 chunks, and onion into 64 pieces. Make pieces uniform in size. Steam the potatoes until just done. Arrange 16 skewers (2 per person) as follows: prawn, onion, potato, basil leaf, scallop, onion, mushroom, basil leaf, prawn, onion, potato, basil leaf, scallop, onion, mushroom, basil leaf. Heat the broth and oil together and brush on the skewered food.

When the coals on the barbecue are ash-white, wet the remaining basil thoroughly and shake off excess water. Make a 2-inch bed of the basil on top of the grill, 6 inches from the coals. Place the skewers on top of the basil and cover with a tent of foil. Grill for 10 minutes, turn, and grill for another 5 minutes. Remove any charred basil leaves and serve with Aioli Sauce.

Aioli Sauce with Sun-dried Tomatoes and Opal Basil

2 tablespoons mayonnaise
1/2 cup nonfat milk
4 garlic cloves, finely minced
2 tablespoons opal basil, finely chopped
4 teaspoons sun-dried tomatoes, minced
2 small baking-type potatoes, or 1 large (about 5 ounces)

Whisk together the mayonnaise and milk, and add the garlic, basil, and sun-dried tomatoes. Peel the potato and boil it until tender. Drain well and mash with a fork until fluffy and smooth (do not use a food processor or blender or the potato may become thick and gummy). Blend the mayonnaise mixture into the potato a bit at a time, and mix well. Drizzle about 1 tablespoon sauce over each skewer of seafood.

GRILLED HERBES DE PROVENCE SALMON FILLET SANDWICHES

Serves 6

Well-flavored grilled fish sandwiches make a hearty, informal midday meal or Sunday supper. The secret to perfect fish is a long marinating time and a very hot grill or skillet.

6 four-ounce boneless salmon fillets (about 1 1/2 pounds)
3 tablespoons olive oil
3 tablespoons fresh lemon juice
2 1/2 teaspoons herbes de Provence
1/2 teaspoon salt
1/4 teaspoon white pepper
Oil to brush pan
6 two-ounce rolls, split

Place the salmon fillets in a single layer in a dish. Combine the oil, lemon juice, herbs, salt, and pepper. Rub the salmon with this marinade. Cover and refrigerate for at least 30 minutes, or as long as overnight, turning once.

Heat a barbecue, indoor griddle, or large frying pan until very hot, and brush with oil. Cook the salmon for 4 minutes, then turn and cook 3 to 4 minutes longer, just until opaque throughout. Serve hot on split rolls spread with Herbes de Provence Lemon-Chive Mayonnaise.

Herbes de Provence Lemon-Chive Mayonnaise

1/2 cup mayonnaise
2 tablespoons chopped fresh chives
1 teaspoon herbes de Provence
2 teaspoons fresh lemon juice

Combine all ingredients and divide among the six rolls.

REDFISH WITH HERB PESTO AND CREAM SAUCE

Serves 6

Herb Pesto

1 cup chopped fresh spinach
1/2 cup chopped fresh basil leaves
1 garlic clove, minced
3 tablespoons fresh grated parmesan cheese
1¹/₂ tablespoons olive oil
2 tablespoons chicken broth
2 tablespoons chopped fresh cilantro

In a blender or food processor, combine all ingredients and puree to a smooth texture. Refrigerate several hours or overnight.

Cream Sauce

1/2 cup ricotta cheese (part skim or low-fat)
2 tablespoons nonfat milk
2 tablespoons nonfat yogurt
1/8 teaspoon salt
1 tablespoon fresh thyme leaves, minced
1 tablespoon sherry
1/4 teaspoon white pepper

In a blender or food processor, puree all ingredients and refrigerate several hours or overnight.

2 8-ounce bottles clam juice or nectar
1 cup white wine
1/3 cup white wine vinegar
3 tablespoons chopped shallots
1/4 cup chopped fresh parsley
24 ounces redfish (or substitute red snapper)
6 carrots

Steam the carrots until fork tender. Meanwhile, bring the clam juice, wine, vinegar, shallots, and parsley to a boil in a large frying pan and add the fish. Reduce heat and simmer for 5–10 minutes, depending on thickness, until fish is opaque all the way through.

Gently reheat the two sauces separately in a double boiler or microwave; avoid high heat as they may curdle. Place one-sixth of the Cream Sauce on each plate, cover with a piece of fish, and top with the pesto; place a carrot alongside each serving of fish.

CRAB CAKES DE PROVENCE

Makes 6 cakes

The herbs that make up a typical herbes de Provence blend—thyme, fennel, oregano—are right at home with seafood.

2 tablespoons butter
1/4 cup finely chopped scallions
1/4 cup finely chopped fresh parsley
1/2 cup unseasoned dry bread crumbs
1 tablespoon Dijon-style mustard
1 teaspoon worcestershire sauce
1 teaspoon herbes de Provence
1 garlic clove, minced
1/8 teaspoon white pepper
6 ounces fresh crab meat (or good-quality canned crab that has been drained and rinsed)
1 egg, beaten
2 egg whites, beaten until frothy

Melt the butter in a skillet and sauté the scallions and parsley over medium-high heat for 3 minutes, stirring often. Reduce heat to low and add the remaining ingredients except the crab and eggs. Cook 3 minutes longer, stirring gently to keep the mixture light. Remove from heat and let cool until lukewarm. Gently fold in the crab and beaten egg, then the beaten egg whites.

Lightly shape this mixture into six cakes. Heat a skillet or griddle over medium-high heat and melt the butter. Sauté the crab cakes for 5 minutes on each side. Serve hot with sauce.

Sauce

6 tablespoons mayonnaise
2 tablespoons chopped fresh parsley
1/4 teaspoon herbes de Provence
1/16 teaspoon cayenne pepper

Mix all ingredients together.

POULTRY, MEAT, AND SEAFOOD

Crab Cakes de Provence with a creamy sauce, recipe opposite.

SMOKED TROUT WITH SAVORY

Makes 4 smoked trout

Smoking is a relatively simple process that we seem content to have given over to commercial food processors, though it works especially well with the rather bland and inexpensive aquacultured trout available in most supermarkets. Because prepared smoked trout is an expensive treat, and because commercially smoked fish is too often dry and overly salty, it is worth knowing how to smoke your own.

If you have a covered barbecue grill, you don't need a smoker to smoke small fish or pieces of meat. The advantage of a smoker is that the heat is easily regulated so that food can be completely cured without drying out. With proper brining and attention to the temperature of the coals, very acceptable smoked fish—and chicken breast—can be produced with the method described below. The caveats are two: do not attempt to smoke pieces of meat or fish heavier than 1 pound in a covered grill, and do eat the smoked foods within two weeks.

4 large trout, about 12 ounces each
1/3 cup plus 2 tablespoons kosher salt
8 to 10 four-inch sprigs winter savory

Rinse the trout very well. Dissolve 1/3 cup kosher salt in 1 gallon of water in a nonreactive container large enough to hold the trout. Place the trout in the brine and refrigerate for at least 6 hours, or as long as overnight.

Rinse the fish and pat very dry. Crush the leaves of four or five savory sprigs with 2 tablespoons kosher salt. Rub the fish well inside and out with this herbed salt. Cover and marinate, refrigerated, at least 6 hours, or overnight.

Hang the fish out of direct sunlight in a place where no insects can touch them. Air-dry them until no liquid drips from them and they are dry to the touch. This may take from two to six hours, depending on heat and humidity. A fan placed 3 or 4 feet in front of the fish speeds the drying process.

If you have a smoker, hang the fish from the hooks, which should pierce the skin and flesh just above the tail, and then suspend them from a bar or rack. An alternative is to pierce the fish with a small sharp knife, thread them onto a foot or so of kitchen twine or unwaxed dental floss, and tie them to a bar or, lacking that, a coat hanger.

To smoke the fish in a smoker, follow the manufacturer's directions. To smoke them in a covered barbecue grill, be sure the grill rack is clean, then use untreated wood charcoal to make a fire large enough to cover the bottom of the grill. Soak 2 cups of smoking chips in 1 quart of hot water while the charcoal is heating. When the charcoal shows red on the bottom, damp the grill by closing the air vents. Let the fire burn for 10 minutes or so, then check the temperature: it should read 250° F on a thermometer. If you do not have a thermometer, hold your hand over the coals 4 inches above the grill rack. You should be able to hold it there for 15 seconds before you have to move it away.

Rub the grill rack well with an oiled paper towel. Add a handful of smoking chips and a branch or two of savory to the coals. Place the air-dried fish, thickest parts over the hottest coals, on the grill rack. Cover the grill.

Check the fish two or three times during the first 15 minutes to be sure that they are not cooking/smoking too quickly. If they are browning or sizzling, remove them for a few minutes while the coals burn down.

The fish will take about an hour and 15 minutes to cook and smoke completely. Add the rest of the smoking chips and savory at intervals. To check whether the fish are done, make a small slit in the thick part of the back just below the gills.

Remove the fish to a clean rack to cool completely to room temperature. Store in the refrigerator, tightly wrapped in plastic wrap or in sealable plastic bags, for as long as two weeks.

*B*aking with herbs

Homemade Herb Breads

Hail to the first unknown baker who added herbs to bread dough! Whether in simple country loaves or refined egg breads, the harmonious blending of aromatics with familiar and exotic grains, nuts, and cheeses ushers in a new world of warm colors, flavors, and textures.

No one can resist the soul-nourishing pleasures of a well-made loaf of bread. It has a chewy, yeasty quality paired with the striking yet subtle flavor of grain. And the possible variations in both form and flavor are virtually endless. Different grains, herbs, and blending techniques produce different textures, colors, aromas, and flavors; and bread dough can be shaped in a loaf container, flattened out on a pizza pan, cut into biscuit shapes, allowed to assume its own natural shape, or formed like modeling clay into braids, pretzels, other interesting forms.

No esoteric knowledge is needed for baking bread; just a light touch and a whimsical, creative spirit. A few simple rules will ensure successful loaves every time you bake.

Always use ingredients of the highest quality. If you're a beginner or occasional baker, be assured that practice will sharpen your instincts. For example, only hands-on experience can tell you when your dough has just the right amount of flour. Too little, and the dough will be too soft to support its shape; too much, and the dough will be tough and hard to knead and will yield a dry finished loaf.

Liquids hotter than 140° F will kill the yeast; those below 100° F will slow the rising process. Rely on a thermometer to keep liquid temperatures comfortably between 100° and 115° F if you question your instincts.

THE HERBS

If you grow your own, you can have fresh herbs available much of the year. Any surpluses can be dried or frozen for use during the rest of the year. If you have no space in your garden to plant herbs, consider pots or an oak barrel. Of course, fresh herbs may also be purchased in many grocery stores.

Fresh herbs seem to have stronger fragrance and milder flavor than their dried counterparts.

The scent and flavor of fresh ones are sharp and bright, while those of dried herbs are warm and mellow. In a recipe, one tablespoon of fresh herbs is about equal to one teaspoon of dried, but let your own palate be your guide, keeping in mind that herbs are more effective as a tantalizing whisper than a dominating flavor.

Three good ways for integrating herbs into homemade bread are 1) kneading chopped fresh or dried herbs into the dough; 2) brushing the tops with an herb-infused oil before or after baking; and 3) baking on a bed of aromatic branches, such as rosemary, thyme, or fennel. The last is especially nice for flat breads cooked on an outdoor grill. Three tablespoons per two loaves is a generous amount of fresh herbs to add to any bread; of dried herbs, use half that amount or less.

Which herbs go best in bread? Embellish as your nature dictates: choose delicate, balmy dill; warm, bold oregano; or the assertive perfume of tarragon. Any herb whose flavor you like is a candidate for use in bread. When mixing herbs, remember to use less of the stronger- and more of the weaker-flavored ones.

WALNUT AND HERB BATTER BREAD

Makes one 9-inch round loaf

This quick, no-knead yeast bread is excellent with Italian food, and all kinds of soups and salads. The nutty flavor goes well with a semisoft cheese such as Gouda, Provolone, or Fontina.

1^1/$_2$ packages (1^1/$_2$ tablespoons) active dry yeast
Pinch sugar
1 cup warm water (105° to 115° F)
1 cup warm milk (105° to 115° F)
2 tablespoons brown sugar
1 tablespoon salt
3 tablespoons chopped fresh parsley
2 tablespoons chopped fresh basil or 1^1/$_2$ teaspoons dried basil
1 tablespoon chopped fresh tarragon or 1^1/$_2$ teaspoons dried tarragon
1 clove garlic, minced
4^1/$_2$ cups unbleached all-purpose flour
3/4 cup walnuts, coarsely chopped

In a small bowl, sprinkle yeast and sugar over warm water. Stir to dissolve and let stand until foamy, about 10 minutes.

Combine milk, sugar, salt, parsley, basil, tarragon, garlic, and 1^1/$_2$ cups flour, and beat until smooth. Add yeast mixture. Add remaining 3 cups flour and beat vigorously by hand or in the electric mixer until batter is smooth yet sticky. Cover with plastic wrap and let rise in a warm place until doubled, about 45 minutes to an hour.

Sprinkle walnuts over the top of the batter and stir down, beating vigorously to distribute the nuts. Turn batter into a well-greased 1^1/$_2$ -quart casserole, soufflé dish, or 9-inch springform pan. Let rise, loosely covered, in a warm place until batter is even with top of pan. Bake in a preheated 375° F oven until brown, crusty, and a cake tester comes out clean, 50 to 60 minutes. Turn loaf out of pan or remove springform sides, and let loaf cool on a rack.

WHOLE WHEAT ONION & HERB BREAD

Makes two loaves

Adding sautéed onions and herbs to this whole wheat loaf lifts it into the realm of the extraordinary. It is a good keeper and makes scrumptious sandwiches.

1/2 cup warm water
1 teaspoon sugar
1 tablespoon dry yeast

Mix and let stand, uncovered, for 10 minutes.

2 cups warm water
2 tablespoons honey
1 tablespoon salt
1 medium onion, finely chopped
2 tablespoons vegetable oil
1 teaspoon sage (dried)
1 teaspoon savory (dried)
3^1/$_2$ cups whole wheat flour
3 to 3^1/$_2$ cups white flour

Sauté onion in salad oil until transparent, then cool. Combine in a large bowl the yeast mixture and warm water, then stir in honey, salt, and herbs. Add whole wheat flour and mix well, then mix in the onions and oil. Add white flour gradually until you can turn the dough out of the bowl for kneading. Work in white flour a little at a time until the dough seems right:

BREADS

Walnut and Herb Batter Bread, recipe opposite.

not too sticky, but moist.

Put the dough in a covered bowl to rise at about 70° F. When it has doubled in bulk, punch it down, divide it into two loaves, shape, and put into greased 8" by 4" by 2½ " pans. Let rise until double and bake at 400° F for 15 minutes. Reduce heat to 350° F and bake for approximately 30 more minutes. Turn out of pans, lightly oil tops, and let cool on a wire rack.

Winter Squash Herb Bread

This savory loaf presents a pairing of herbs that is rarely seen but interestingly compatible. Adventurous cooks will undoubtedly want to pursue the combination of sage and dill, with or without the healthy dose of garlic, in recipes other than bread.

1/2 cup milk
1/4 cup butter or margarine
2 tablespoons sugar
1 tablespoon baking yeast
1/4 cup warm water
3 cups unbleached flour
2 eggs, lightly beaten
1 cup finely grated winter squash
2 tablespoons finely chopped fresh or 1 tablespoon
  dried sage
1 tablespoon finely chopped fresh or 1/2 tablespoon
  dried dill weed
4 cloves garlic, crushed
1 teaspoon salt

Combine the milk, butter, and sugar in a small saucepan and heat, stirring, until the butter is melted. Remove from heat and set aside.

In a large mixing bowl, dissolve the yeast in the warm water. Add 2 cups of flour and the eggs, squash, sage, dill, garlic, and salt. Mix slightly to combine ingredients. When the milk mixture has cooled to lukewarm, stir it in with the rest of the ingredients to form a sticky ball.

Add the remaining flour 1/3 cup at a time, mixing to moisten each addition, until the dough becomes smooth. It will be wet and slightly sticky. Cover your hands with a little flour, turn the dough out onto a lightly floured surface, and knead briefly.

Form the dough into a ball and place in a lightly greased loaf pan. It can also be divided into small balls to make dinner rolls (place on a lightly greased cookie sheet or in a muffin tin). Cover with plastic wrap and let rise until the dough has more than doubled, about 1 to 1½ hours. While the dough is rising, preheat oven to 275° F.

Place the risen dough in the oven and bake until the top is golden brown and the sides slightly brown, an hour or 70 minutes. Check the sides by pulling the bread out of the pan. When done, cool bread on a wire rack, then serve or wrap and refrigerate.

Tomato Basil Baguette

Makes 2 baguettes

The words "French bread" conjure up the image of a long, skinny loaf with a crisp, crackly crust and soft-textured interior dotted with irregular holes—the ubiquitous baguette. A baker's repertoire would be incomplete without it. Crusty Tomato Basil Baguettes are quick to assemble and bake, and they boast an irresistible incenselike aroma.

These baguettes make superb sandwiches. Try any and all of the following fillings: ricotta, fresh basil leaves, and thin slices of yellow plum tomatoes; mozzarella and anchovy strips browned under the broiler; tomato paste and gorgonzola melt; turkey breast, sweet butter, and sprouts. Add cold kir to drink, an artichoke-and-sprout salad, and a truffle for dessert, and you have the makings of a truly decadent picnic.

This dough can also be transformed into a 16-inch party pizza. After flattening it in the pan, brush the dough with extra-virgin olive oil, coat with a thin layer of tomato sauce, and top with cheeses.

3 cups unbleached all-purpose or bread flour
1/4 cup nonfat powdered dry milk
12 fresh basil leaves, minced, or 1 tablespoon dried basil
1½ teaspoons salt
3 tablespoons soft butter
1 tablespoon active dry yeast
1/4 cup lukewarm water (110° F)
Pinch sugar
2/3 cup lukewarm water (110° F)
1/3 cup tomato paste
1 tablespoon egg plus 1 teaspoon water for brushing
  top of loaves

Combine flour, powdered milk, basil, and salt in a large bowl or the work bowl of a heavy-duty electric mixer. Cut in butter until mixture resembles coarse meal.

Combine yeast, 1/4 cup lukewarm water, and sugar in a large measuring cup. Set aside about 10 minutes, or until foamy. Combine 2/3 cup lukewarm water with tomato paste and add to yeast mixture. Make a well in the flour and pour in liquid. Stir to mix thoroughly. Knead by hand or machine about 5 minutes, or until dough is smooth and elastic. Place in a well-greased large mixing bowl, cover with plastic wrap, and set in a warm place to rise until doubled in bulk, about 1½ hours.

Turn dough out onto a well-floured surface. Knead lightly and form into a smooth ball and roll out to form a 14-by-7-inch rectangle. Cut the rectangle in two lengthwise. Roll each piece up tightly, starting with one of the long sides, and place diagonally on a greased cookie sheet. Brush with egg/water mixture and slash top diagonally. Cover loosely and let rise until doubled, about 40 minutes.

Bake loaves in preheated 375° F oven until golden brown, about 30 to 35 minutes. Cool on a rack. Don't slice until the loaf is cool enough to handle.

ROSEMARY AND OREGANO FOCACCIA

The Italian bread best known in the United States is certainly pizza, but it is just one in a family of ancient Italian flat breads that are customarily made at home as well as in bakeries. Focaccia is basic pizza dough pressed onto a baking sheet and topped with a coating of olive oil and herbs or garlic. It is served as a tender, fragrant snack or as bread. Focaccia can be made any size. Sometimes, the dough is sliced through down the center (but not through the edges) to make decorative braided or ropelike patterns. Cut horizontally, it makes a wonderful sandwich bread, perfect for picnics. Focaccia is also known as schiacciata and, in France, as fougasse.

One recipe focaccia dough (see below)
Cornmeal, for sprinkling
1/3 cup extra virgin olive oil
1¼ teaspoons dried rosemary
1 teaspoon dried leaf oregano

Prepare focaccia dough and let rise. If dough has been refrigerated, it may take about 2 hours to come to room temperature and rise.

Place dough ball on a work surface. Use heel of hand to press and flatten dough. Lift and gently pull dough, stretching to fit an oiled and cornmeal-sprinkled 11-by-7-by-1-inch jelly roll pan. Cover gently with plastic wrap and let rise in a warm place until doubled in bulk, 30 minutes to an hour.

Meanwhile, combine olive oil and herbs. Let stand 30 minutes. Place baking tiles or pizza stone on lowest rack of a cold oven and preheat at 450° to 500° F for about 30 minutes.

With fingertips or knuckle, gently poke some indentations in the surface of the dough. Drizzle herb oil over dough, letting it pool in the indentations.

Reduce oven temperature to 400° F. Bake on hot tiles 20 to 30 minutes, or until nicely browned. Serve warm from the oven.

Focaccia Dough

Makes eight 6-inch rounds or one 11-by-17-inch rectangle
4 teaspoons active dry yeast
Pinch sugar, honey, or malt extract
2 cups warm water (105° to 115° F)
1 teaspoon salt
About 5 cups unbleached all-purpose or bread flour
1/4 cup extra virgin olive oil

In a two-cup measure, sprinkle yeast and sugar over water and let stand until dissolved and foamy, about 10 minutes.

In a large bowl or the work bowl of a heavy-duty electric mixer, combine salt and 3 cups flour. Stir in yeast mixture and olive oil and beat hard 3 minutes. Add flour, 1/2 cup at a time, until dough clears the sides of the bowl.

On a lightly floured surface, knead to form a springy ball, adding only 1 tablespoon flour at a time as needed to prevent sticking. Dough will remain very moist and pliable. Place dough in an oiled bowl, cover with plastic wrap, and let rise until doubled or tripled in bulk, 1 to 1½ hours. You may also let dough rise, then punch down and place the bowl, well covered, in refrigerator for up to two days before baking. (You'll probably need to punch it down once more a couple of hours after refrigerating.)

Dough Variations
—Whole wheat focaccia: Substitute 2½ cups whole wheat flour for 2½ cups unbleached flour.
—Cornmeal focaccia: Substitute 1 cup yellow cornmeal or polenta for 1 cup unbleached flour.
—Garlic focaccia: Add 3 cloves minced fresh garlic to the dough during mixing.
—Bran focaccia: Substitute 3/4 cup whole wheat flour and 1/2 cup wheat bran or oat bran for an equal amount of unbleached flour.
—Semolina focaccia: Substitute 1 cup semolina flour for 1 cup unbleached flour for a flavorful, grainy texture.
—Herb focaccia: Add 1/2 to 2/3 cup chopped fresh herbs (such as basil, tarragon, chervil, oregano, marjoram, parsley) to the dough during mixing.
—Saffron focaccia: Add 1/2 teaspoon saffron threads to 2 cups boiling water. Let water cool to temperature called for in recipe before adding to yeast.

BREADSTICKS WITH
BLACK PEPPER AND CHEDDAR

Makes twenty 1-by-12-inch breadsticks

More like small baguettes than the completely dry commercial breadsticks, these have a crisp crust and a chewy, bready interior. They have a nice, lingering, peppery aftertaste that complements most soups and salads, and aperitifs or cocktails.

2¹/₂ cups unbleached flour plus about 1/2 cup for
*   kneading*
1/2 cup whole wheat flour
1¹/₂ teaspoons salt
1¹/₂ tablespoons active dry yeast
Generous pinch sugar
1¹/₂ cups warm water
2 tablespoons vegetable oil
2 teaspoons coarsely ground black pepper
3 green onions, sliced thin (about 1/4 cup)
1 cup grated cheddar cheese
1 egg white lightly beaten with 1 teaspoon water
Kosher salt, optional

In a mixing bowl, combine 1¹/₂ cups of the un-bleached flour with the whole wheat flour and salt. Make a well in the flour and add the yeast, sugar, and 1/2 cup of the warm water. Let the yeast stand until foamy, about 5 to 10 minutes.

Stir in another 1/2 cup water and the oil. Add the remaining water, and stir the batter vigorously with a wooden spoon. Add 1/2 cup flour and beat well. Stir in the pepper, scallions, cheese, and another 1/2 cup flour and blend well.

Sprinkle about 1/4 cup of the flour for kneading on a pastry board or marble and turn the dough out onto it. Knead, adding the rest of the flour as need-ed, until the dough is smooth and homogeneous and springs back when pressed with your thumb. The dough will be slightly sticky, but should not be too sticky. Add a bit more flour if necessary.

Cover the dough with a clean, dry tea towel and let it rest 5 to 10 minutes. Roll it into a cylinder about 20 to 24 inches long and cut the cylinder into about 20 pieces with a sharp knife. Let the pieces rest, cov-ered, for 5 minutes.

Lightly oil two baking sheets and sprinkle them lightly with cornmeal. Roll each piece of dough into a cylinder about 10 inches long and 3/4 inch wide, and place ten of them on each baking sheet. If you prefer smaller breadsticks, cut each one in half cross-wise.

Preheat the oven to 350° F and set the baking sheets, covered with clean tea towels, in a warm place to rise. Gas ovens generate a warmth while preheat-ing which is just right for raising the dough; just turn the baking sheets occasionally to ensure even heat. If you have an electric oven, choose a different place for raising. Let the sticks rise 25 to 30 minutes, until they have increased in size by about 50 percent.

With a sharp knife, make five or six diagonal slash-es on top of each breadstick. Brush them lightly with the egg white and water mixture. Sprinkle very light-ly with the salt, if desired.

Bake the breadsticks for 20 to 25 minutes (16 to 20 minutes if you've cut them in half), changing the position of the baking sheets on the oven racks about halfway through baking time. The breadsticks should be golden brown. Eat them right away or let them cool and store them in tightly closed tins; wrapped tightly, they can be stored in the freezer for up to a month.

ITALIAN RICOTTA AND
PARSLEY BRAID

Makes one 12-inch loaf

This delectable Italian bread features a surprise fill-ing of piquant fresh parsley. It's based on an ancient dish called torta d'erbe: a savory, rustic herb pie filled with ricotta, parmesan cheese, and eggs and remi-niscent of its French cousin, the quiche. Beet greens, swiss chard, spinach, borage, and sorrel have been the traditional tangy "erbe" in the filling since me-dieval times. For a memorable picnic, serve the braid with a fresh, cool salad and fresh fruit.

Dough

1¹/₂ tablespoons active dry yeast
Pinch sugar
1/4 cup warm milk (105° to 115° F)
1¹/₂ cups ricotta cheese
2 large eggs
1¹/₂ teaspoons salt
6 tablespoons (3/4 stick) unsalted butter, melted and
*   cooled*
4 to 4¹/₂ cups unbleached all-purpose or bread flour

Filling

1 cup ricotta cheese
1 egg
1/4 cup freshly grated parmesan cheese
1 teaspoon dried basil
1 teaspoon dried oregano
2 tablespoons minced fresh parsley leaves

In a small bowl, sprinkle yeast and sugar over the milk. Stir to dissolve and let stand at room temperature for 15 minutes or until foamy.

In a large bowl, or in the work bowl of a heavy-duty electric mixer, combine ricotta, salt, and butter. Add 1½ cups flour and the yeast mixture, then beat until smooth, about 2 minutes. Add flour, 1/2 cup at a time, until the soft dough clears the sides of the bowl. Turn out dough onto a lightly floured surface and knead until it is smooth and firm, yet springy. The texture will be slightly dense, owing to the presence of the cheese. Add enough flour so the dough can hold its own shape, but not more than 4½ cups total. Transfer dough to a greased bowl and let rise, covered loosely with plastic wrap, in a warm place until doubled in bulk, 1½ to 2 hours.

While dough is rising, prepare the filling by combining all ingredients in a small bowl. Beat well until smooth and refrigerate until needed.

Gently deflate dough and divide it into three equal portions. Roll each into a 14-by-4-inch rectangle. Spread 1/3 of the filling down the center of each rectangle, leaving a 1-inch border all around. Fold the dough over lengthwise and pinch the edges together to enclose the filling completely. Lay the three strips parallel on a parchment-lined baking sheet. Braid the dough gently and tuck the ends under. Cover loosely with plastic wrap and let the braid rise in a warm place for 45 minutes to an hour, or until doubled in bulk.

Bake braid in an oven preheated to 375° F until it is golden and a cake tester poked into the center comes out clean. Remove from pan and let cool on rack before slicing.

CRUSTY PROVENÇAL HERB ROLLS

Makes 2 dozen dinner or 16 sandwich rolls

It's been said that food is as much an art as music or painting in sun-baked Provence, in the south of France. Provençal cooks use the wild herbs that cover the rocky, rolling hills to give the region's cuisine its pungent, complex character. These simple French rolls contain a lusty blend of those herbs (herbes de Provence) reinforced with extra lavender and basil. You can create your own herbes de Provence by mixing five or more of the following: thyme, sage, fennel, rosemary, basil, oregano, lavender, and mint. If you buy a commercial blend at a specialty grocery, it's better to buy one that's produced domestically; herbs imported from Europe often are old or of low quality.

These rolls are delicious served hot with a platter of roasted vegetables and aioli.

2 teaspoons dried herbes de Provence
2 teaspoons fresh lavender flowers or 1 teaspoon dried flowers
2 teaspoons fresh chopped basil or 3/4 teaspoon dried basil
1/4 cup olive oil
5½ to 6 cups unbleached all-purpose or bread flour
1½ tablespoons active dry yeast
1 tablespoon sugar
1 tablespoon salt
1²/₃ cups warm water (105° to 115° F)
1/2 cup orange muscat dessert wine, such as Essenia

Combine herbs in a small bowl with olive oil and let stand 1 hour at room temperature to soften.

In a large mixing bowl, or in the work bowl of a heavy-duty electric mixer fitted with the paddle attachment, combine 2½ cups of flour, yeast, sugar, salt, and the herb/oil mixture. Add water and wine. Beat on medium speed or with a whisk until smooth, about 1 minute. On low speed, add remaining flour, 1/2 cup at a time, to make a shaggy dough that clears the sides of the bowl.

Turn dough out onto a lightly floured surface and knead, adding 1 tablespoon flour at a time until it becomes smooth, silky, and resilient, about 3 minutes. This dough will not be sticky.

Place dough in a greased bowl and turn once to grease top. Cover with plastic wrap and let rise at warm room temperature until doubled in bulk, about 50 to 60 minutes.

Gently deflate dough and turn out onto work surface. Divide it into 24 equal portions for dinner rolls or 16 for sandwich rolls. The best way to do this is to divide in half three times, then divide each piece into either two or three equal portions. Work the dough as little as possible; too much handling will make it too springy to form, and you'll have to cover it and let it relax for 10 minutes or so.

Roll each piece into a tight, round ball. Place rolls about 2 inches apart on parchment-lined baking sheets. Pinch ends to elongate slightly into a navette, or weaver's shuttle . Cover loosely with plastic wrap and let rest about 15 minutes while preheating oven to 425° F.

Pinch ends again and, with a sharp knife, slash the top of each roll to allow for expansion while baking. Place pans in preheated oven and bake until golden brown and crusty, 15 to 18 minutes. Change positions of the pans about halfway through baking. Serve immediately or freeze for later.

HERBAL CITRUS SCONES

Makes 8 scones

2 cups unbleached all-purpose flour
2 teaspoons baking powder
1/2 teaspoon salt
2 tablespoons sugar
1/4 cup butter, slightly softened
2 eggs, beaten
1/3 cup milk or light cream
2 tablespoons herbs (lemon balm, basil, mint, or sage),
  minced
Grated zest of 1 orange
Grated zest of 1 lemon or lime

Preheat the oven to 425° F. Lightly grease a baking sheet.

Combine the flour, baking powder, salt, and sugar in a mixing bowl. Cut in the butter until the dough resembles coarse meal. Stir in the eggs, then fold in the milk, herbs, and citrus zest.

With a melon baller or large spoon, drop the dough onto the baking sheet. Press the blobs lightly with the palm of your hand to smooth and slightly flatten, and leave about 2 inches between them. Bake for 10 to 12 minutes, or until the crusts are light brown. Serve hot or at room temperature, with a hot beverage or milk.

RASPBERRY MINT MUFFINS

Makes 10 large or 18 medium muffins

2 cups unbleached all-purpose flour
2 teaspoons baking powder
1/2 teaspoon salt
1/2 cup butter
3/4 cup white sugar
1/2 cup brown sugar
2 eggs
1 teaspoon vanilla
1/2 cup milk
2¹/₂ cups raspberries or blueberries
1/4 cup mint leaves, finely chopped

Preheat the oven to 375° F. In a large mixing bowl, combine flour, baking powder, and salt. In a separate mixing bowl, cream the butter. Add the sugar to the butter and cream at high speed. Add the eggs one at a time, creaming after each, then add vanilla and cream again. Add half the milk, then half the dry ingredients, then the rest of the milk, then the rest of the dry ingredients. Mix after each addition, but only enough to wet the dry ingredients.

Mash 2 cups of the berries by hand and mix them into the batter, then fold the remaining whole berries and mint leaves into the mix. Spoon the batter into greased muffin tins. Bake for 25 to 35 minutes, until a toothpick inserted in the center comes out clean. Cool for 10 minutes in the pan, then remove the muffins and allow to cool on a rack.

LEMON VERBENA MUFFINS

Of all the lemon herbs, lemon verbena has the most pronounced and, to many palates, the most pleasing flavor. The shrub, a native of South America, grows well outside in the warmer parts of the United States and can be grown in cooler climates if it is brought inside for the winter.

This recipe can be used for madeleines if you have the traditional shell-shaped madeleine pans. The muffins, made in miniature muffin pans, are pleasantly firm.

1 cup butter, softened
2¹/₂ cups sifted powdered sugar
4 eggs at room temperature
2 cups all-purpose flour
1 teaspoon grated lemon zest
1 tablespoon lemon verbena leaves, clean, dry, and
  finely chopped

With an electric mixer, beat butter until fluffy, then gradually beat in sugar. Add eggs one at a time, beating at high speed after each addition. Add lemon zest and lemon verbena leaves, mixing thoroughly after each addition.

Spoon 1 tablespoon batter into each cup of a buttered muffin pan and bake at 350° F for 20 to 25 minutes or until lightly browned. Remove muffins from pan immediately and cool on a rack. Dust lightly with powdered sugar and serve warm or at room temperature.

These muffins can be frozen ahead of time and thawed on the way to the picnic.

BUTTERMILK CREAM SCONES WITH LEMON BALM

Makes about 2 dozen

These scones combine the tender texture of a cream scone and the tangy flavor of a buttermilk scone. Strawberry is the recommended jam for scones, but raspberry, lingonberry, and gooseberry are delicious, too.

Raspberry Mint Muffins and Herbal Citrus Scones, recipes opposite.

The proper way to eat a scone is to split it in half, spread each half with jam, then top each with a generous dollop of whipped cream. The cream should be just barely sweetened with vanilla sugar and whipped until thick, but not stiff.

2 1/4 cups unbleached white flour
2 teaspoons sugar
3/4 teaspoon salt
2 teaspoons baking powder
1/2 teaspoon baking soda
4 tablespoons unsalted butter
1/2 cup buttermilk
1/2 cup cream
2 tablespoons freshly chopped lemon balm
1 1/2 teaspoons lemon zest, finely chopped

Preheat oven to 425° F. Combine the dry ingredients in a large bowl and blend thoroughly. Cut in the butter until the mixture resembles coarse meal.

Stir the buttermilk and cream together with the lemon balm and zest. Add the liquid to the dry ingredients and stir to form a soft dough.

Turn the dough onto a floured pastry marble or board, knead gently until it just comes together, and roll out to 1/2-inch thickness. Cut the dough with a 1 3/4 – or 2-inch cookie cutter and place on an ungreased baking sheet.

Bake the scones for 10 to 12 minutes or until golden brown. Remove to baking rack and cool slightly before serving. The scones are best served warm and right after baking. If you are preparing them in advance, cool them completely and store in an airtight container. Wrap them in foil and gently reheat them in a 325 degree F oven for 10 to 15 minutes.

FRESH SAGE MUFFINS

Makes 12 muffins

Savory rather than sweet muffins are an unusual idea and a delightful change from ordinary dinner rolls or bread. These sage- and parsley-studded muffins are a wonderful complement to any meal, and they make a wonderful snack or light lunch when paired with cheese and a salad. Try baking them in miniature muffin cups and serving them as an unusual hors d'oeuvre.

2 cups flour
2 teaspoons sugar
2 teaspoons baking powder
1/2 teaspoon salt
1 cup milk

1 egg
1/4 cup butter, melted
1/2 cup finely chopped fresh sage
1/2 cup chopped fresh parsley

Combine flour, sugar, baking powder, and salt. Mix milk with egg, butter, sage, and parsley. Combine with dry ingredients, mixing just enough to moisten. (Overmixing results in heavy muffins.) Pour into 12 muffin cups sprayed with cooking spray or fitted with paper cupcake liners. Bake in a preheated 400° F oven for 20 to 25 minutes or until top springs back when touched.

THYME AND SCALLION CORN MUFFINS

Makes 12 muffins

This is an herbal version of a Southern specialty. These muffins make nice companions for soups and salads. Or serve them as an afternoon snack with tea.

1 cup yellow corn meal
1 cup all purpose flour
1/4 cup sugar
3 tablespoons fresh nutmeg thyme or common thyme
1 tablespoon baking powder
1/2 teaspoon salt
1/4 teaspoon black pepper
2 eggs, beaten
1/2 cup buttermilk
1/2 cup milk
1/4 cup melted butter
1/2 cup chopped scallions

Preheat the oven to 375° F. Combine the first seven ingredients in a bowl and mix thoroughly. In a separate bowl, whisk the eggs, buttermilk, milk, and butter together and add the scallions. Fold the liquid ingredients into the dry ingredients, and continue to fold gently until the mixture forms a batter. Divide the batter evenly into a greased 12-muffin pan, or put it all into an 8-inch greased baking pan. Bake for about 20 minutes, or until the crust is lightly brown and a toothpick inserted in the center comes out clean. Serve at once.

ZUCCHINI MADELEINES

Makes one dozen

1 1/2 cups zucchini, shredded
1/2 teaspoon salt
2 eggs

2 tablespoons snipped chives
2 tablespoons snipped parsley
1 tablespoon fresh snipped dill weed
2 tablespoons salad oil
Fresh ground black pepper
1/2 cup buttermilk baking mix
Sandwich filling: chicken or tuna salad or cream cheese

Place the shredded zucchini in a colander and sprinkle with the salt. Place waxed paper over the top of the colander and weight it with a heavy object, then place the colander on a plate or in a bowl in the refrigerator for 30 to 45 minutes. Remove and squeeze the zucchini to remove all moisture.

Place zucchini, eggs, chives, parsley, dill weed, salad oil, and black pepper (to taste) in a bowl and stir to blend well. Add the baking mix and stir just enough to blend. Spoon the mixture into madeleine pans (the larger ones work best). Use a toothpick to stir the batter once it is molded to eliminate any air bubbles. Bake at 350° F for 20 minutes or until puffed and browned. Cool.

Cut the madeleines in half lengthwise and spread with the sandwich filling. Madeleines may be frozen for one month. Bring to room temperature before cutting and filling.

CHEESE TWISTS

Makes about 60 twists

1 cup all-purpose flour
1/4 teaspoon cayenne pepper
1 tablespoon snipped parsley
1 tablespoon snipped chives
1 tablespoon snipped winter savory
1/4 cup cold butter, cut in chunks
1/2 cup (2 ounces) sharp cheddar cheese, finely shredded
1 egg yolk

Preheat oven to 400° F. Grease a large baking sheet. Place the flour, cayenne pepper, parsley, chives, savory, and butter in a food processor and pulse until the mixture is crumbly. Add cheese and egg yolk and pulse several times, then add cold water a teaspoon at a time until a stiff dough is formed. (If you don't have a food processor, cut the butter into the flour and seasonings with two knives or a pastry blender.) Add the cheese, egg yolk, and water with a fork, or use fingers if necessary. Let the dough rest at least one hour, then quarter it and roll it out on a floured surface, one quarter at a time.

Roll the dough 1/4 inch thick and cut into strips 3 inches long by 1/2 inch wide. Transfer the strips to the baking sheet, twisting each strip several times. Bake 10 minutes or until pale golden. Cool on a rack.

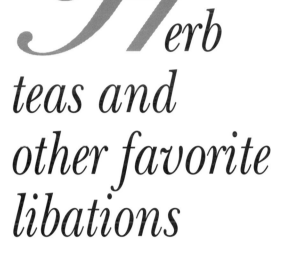

Herb
teas and
other favorite
libations

Herb Teas

The secrets to a fine cup of herb tea are good water brought just to the boil, a heaping teaspoon of dried herbs per cup of water, and five to ten minutes of steeping time.

Many herbs make delightful teas by themselves: sage, rosemary, catnip, chamomile blossoms, mint. There's no end to the possible blends; just check the list of ingredients on some of the fancifully named brews at your local supermarket. Here are some points of departure, each making two to three cups' worth:

1 tablespoon dried sage, 1 teaspoon dried orange peel
1 tablespoon dried rosehips, 1 stick of cinnamon
1 tablespoon dried lemon basil, 1 teaspoon thyme
1 tablespoon dried chamomile flowers, 1 tablespoon dried
apple mint leaves

Herb Garden Special Tea

Mix equal parts dried bergamot, lemon balm, peppermint, and pineapple or orange mint. To prepare tea, pour boiling water over teabag or loose tea, and steep for 5 to 10 minutes. Sweeten with honey if desired.

National Herb Week Tea

Makes 4 cups

National Herb Week, sponsored by the International Herb Association, occurs each year in the first week of May. This is the week's official brew, and is delicious hot or cold.

1 quart water
*2 heaping teaspoons chopped fresh nettle leaves (*Urtica dioica*) or 1 heaping teaspoon dried (wear gloves*
when gathering and preparing fresh nettle leaves)
2 heaping teaspoons chopped fresh spearmint leaves
*(*Mentha spicata*), or 1 heaping teaspoon dried*
2 heaping teaspoons chopped fresh violet leaves and
*flowers (*Viola *sp.), or 1 heaping teaspoon dried*
*1/2 teaspoon dried aniseed (*Pimpinella anisum*),*
slightly crushed
4 fresh strawberries, sliced

Bring the water to a boil. Place the remaining ingredients in a teapot that has been warmed. Pour the boiling water over the herbs, cover, and let steep for 10 minutes. Strain the tea and serve.

A leaf or two of peppermint- or rose-scented geranium, steeped in a pot of regular black tea, provides a delicate hint of flavor.

Preserving Herbs for Tea

The obvious advantage to growing your own tea herbs is that *you* are in control—you can be sure they are free from chemical residues and are picked at their peak of flavor. During the summer, you can make tea from fresh herbs from the garden, but unless you have a greenhouse or live in a very mild climate, winter enjoyment of your own herb teas requires preserving the herbs. Below are several ways of doing that.

DRYING TEA HERBS

The traditional way to preserve herbs is to dry them, and air circulation and a little warmth are usually sufficient. If you apply heat to speed the process, it's important to keep the temperature low enough so the essential oils in the plant won't be released and evaporate along with the moisture. Air temperatures below 90° F are recommended for most herbs, although higher temperatures don't seem to cause a loss of flavor in the faster drying herbs such as lemon balm and monarda. With any artificial drying system, it's important to remove the herbs from the heat source as soon as they are brittle.

THE HANGING METHOD

The traditional drying method is to wash the herb stalks gently, bind them into small bundles—use rubber bands because the bundle contracts as the drying stems shrink—and hang them upside down in a dry, shaded, well-ventilated place. Rodale's *Illustrated Encyclopedia of Herbs* recommends brushing harvested herbs to remove dust and insects because washing dilutes the flavorful oils and adds moisture to something you want to dry as quickly as possible. If you do wash your herbs (which probably removes more dust and insects than brushing will), pat them dry with a towel or spin them in a salad spinner to remove as much moisture as possible.

You don't need an attic or a kitchen with exposed rafters, two traditional places for hanging herbs to dry. Any place with good air circulation will do; a breezeway works nicely. (We've even seen herbs hung to dry in the blast of air from an air conditioner.) If you hang herbs from the rafters of your screened porch, hang the stalks inside paper bags to keep out windblown dust. Cutting small slits in the sides of the paper bags reduces the risk of

TRIPLE MINT TEA

Mix equal parts dried Blue Balsam mint, spearmint, and pineapple mint. To prepare tea, pour boiling water over teabag or loose tea, and steep for 5 to 10 minutes. Sweeten with honey if desired.

MULLED ROSEMARY WINE AND BLACK TEA

Makes about 2 quarts

The aroma of this beverage is inviting, and the punch can be kept warm over very low heat for a few hours, which makes the house smell wonderful. If you have leftovers, remove the oranges and rosemary, let the punch cool to room temperature, then refrigerate. Reheated gently with fresh oranges and rosemary, the punch will be a bit stronger but still quite enjoyable.

1 bottle claret or other full-bodied red wine
1 quart black tea, preferably Assam or Darjeeling
1/4 cup mild honey

1/3 cup sugar, or to taste
2 oranges, sliced thin and seeded
2 three-inch cinnamon sticks
6 whole cloves
3 rosemary sprigs

Pour the wine and tea into a noncorrodible saucepan. Add the honey, sugar, oranges, spices, and rosemary. Heat over low heat until barely steaming. Stir until the honey is dissolved.

Remove the pan from the heat, cover, and let stand for at least 30 minutes. When ready to serve, reheat until just steaming and serve hot.

BLOODY MARY MIX

Serves 4–6

1 large can tomato juice (32 ounces)
6 sorrel leaves, midrib vein removed, or small handful lemon basil
6 long sprigs salad burnet, stems removed, or several cucumber slices

mildew while the bags keep the dust off the herbs.

Hanging herbs near heat-producing appliances such as a water heater, stove, refrigerator, or clothes dryer may speed drying, but plants don't air-dry well anywhere when the relative humidity exceeds about 85 percent. In really humid climates, you'll probably have better success with other drying techniques.

OVEN DRYING

A gas stove with an oven pilot light is a ready-made herb dryer. (Some sensitive noses can detect the odor of gas in oven-dried foods and herbs, but we think this is rare.) Clean the herb leaves, spread them in a thin, loose layer on cookie sheets, and put them in the unlit oven. If your oven is electric, or if your gas oven has electronic ignition, preheat it to the lowest possible setting, *turn it off*, and then put in the cookie sheets of herbs.

Leave the oven door slightly ajar to allow air circulation. You may need to stir or rearrange the herbs (and reheat if there's no pilot light) two or three times for even drying, but the herbs should be crispy-dry in a few days.

USING A FOOD DRYER

If you own an electric food dryer, you probably are drying herbs according to the manufacturer's directions. The controlled air circulation aids quick drying; the closed conditions focus the air flow on the herbs and keep them clean; and the temperature is relatively low (105°–115° F). Most herbs dried in a food dryer come out green, fresh-looking, and flavorful. For more sensitive herbs, such as basil, flavor may be preserved better if the drying process begins with low-temperature air drying, then finishes with the slightly higher temperature (hence faster drying) of a food dryer after partial drying has sealed in the volatile oils.

STORING DRIED HERBS

Dried herbs should be stored in tightly sealed glass jars in a dark place well away from your stove or other heat source. If you want to keep some tea herbs near the stove for convenience, keep only small quantities there so you'll use them up before they deteriorate.

The herbs must be absolutely crisp before you seal them into jars; otherwise, they may mildew. *Camellia sinensis* is intentionally fermented to make oolong or black tea, but a jar of unintentionally fermented tea herbs is not a pretty sight.

6 sprigs basil (cinnamon basil is tasty)
6 or more sprigs cilantro or fresh parsley
1/2 teaspoon crushed dried red pepper
1/2 teaspoon freshly ground black pepper
1/4 teaspoon celery seed
6 tablespoons fresh lime juice
2 tablespoons red wine or sherry vinegar (herb-flavored vinegar is delicious)
Generous splash Worcestershire sauce

Finely mince herbs. Grind the peppers and celery seeds in a spice grinder and add to the herbs along with the lime juice and vinegar; grind this mixture with a mortar and pestle to a slightly thick green sauce. (Alternatively, blend the herbs, spices, lime juice and vinegar to a smooth paste in a food processor.) Pour tomato juice into a glass pitcher and add the herb mixture. Refrigerate overnight; adjust seasonings. Serve garnished with a citrus slice and a fresh herb sprig. For a spirited kick, add a shot of gold tequila, vodka, or gin.

SASSY SANGRIA

20 servings

2 oranges, thinly sliced
1 lemon, thinly sliced
2 limes, thinly sliced
Fresh fruits such as seedless grapes, strawberries, apple slices, pear slices
1 pound package frozen peaches or frozen blueberries
1½–2 cups Grand Marnier liqueur
1½ cups brandy
2 very large bunches fresh herbs such as lemon verbena, lemon balm, mints, Mexican marigold mint, and pineapple sage
1 gallon dry white wine
Sparkling mineral water or champagne (optional)

At least 2 days before serving, mix all ingredients (except frozen fruit and sparkling mineral water or champagne) in a large glass container, twisting the stems of the herbs to release flavor. Just before serving, transfer mixture to a clear glass pitcher or bowl with a fresh bouquet of herbs and the frozen fruit (edible flowers may be used as well). Serve in glasses with herbal ice cubes and a splash of champagne or mineral water and a fresh herb sprig.

Ginger Beer

Makes about 1 gallon

The Swedes make a soft "beer" that's flavored only with lemons; the addition of pungent fresh ginger root makes a refreshing, thirst-quenching beverage. We've seen recipes that also add a sprig or two of rosemary.

1 ounce fresh ginger root, chopped coarsely
1 lemon, thinly sliced
2 cups sugar
1 gallon water
1/8 teaspoon yeast

Place ginger root and lemon slices in a large kettle and bruise them with a potato masher. Add water, bring to a boil, and simmer gently for 30 minutes. Remove from heat, add sugar, and stir until dissolved. Cool to lukewarm. Stir in yeast, and let stand for about an hour. Bottle as described for root beer (next page) and store in a cool place.

Herbal Liqueurs

Humans discovered early that grains, fruits, and vegetables could be fermented to yield alcoholic beverages. They were not long in finding further that these liquids could be distilled for greater potency. A natural evolution of these felicitous practices was the addition of herbs and spices. The result? Some very interesting and tasty combinations: those potables we call liqueurs, cordials, aperitifs, and bitters. Their ingredients are often so great in number and so subtly blended as to be individually unrecognizable, but they suggest interesting possibilities for experimenting, using commercial alcoholic bases and the bounty of our own spice shelves and herb gardens.

Liqueurs and Cordials

The above-mentioned beverages all have in common a relatively high alcoholic content and flavors derived from infusing them with aromatic ingredients. Liqueurs and cordials are generally rather sweet; some are flavored with fruits, nuts, or chocolate, and are suitable complements to, or substitutes for, dessert. The ones we will consider here are flavored with herbs.

Chartreuse, which contain 130 herbs, is the fabled legacy of the French order of Carthusian monks. The order produced a yellow *élixir de table,* as well as the darker and stronger green *élixir de santé.* Green Chartreuse is a spicy, minty, 110-proof liqueur. Yellow Chartreuse, with the same ingredients but mellowed with honey, is only 86 proof. As with other elixirs, this was considered a digestive to be taken not as a beverage, but in little sips at the end of a meal. Both green and yellow Chartreuse are now used as aperitifs, or appetite stimulants, before a meal as well.

Absinthe is another liqueur originally designed as a digestive. It is popular in New Orleans, where it's served with a sugar cube in the traditional manner.

Benedictine is one of the oldest of liqueurs, dating back to 1510 when a Benedictine monk, Dom Bernardo Vincelli, steeped herbs, seeds, and spices in brandy. Among the ingredients found in this elixir are hyssop, thyme, cloves, cinnamon, nutmeg, and myrrh. In the great kitchens of the world, chefs have often referred to Benedictine as "the spice rack in a bottle"; it is used to enhance everything from appetizers to desserts. Unlike fruit-, nut-, or cream-based liqueurs, Benedictine has a subtle, complex flavor, a result of the skillful blending and balancing of a wide variety of ingredients.

Bitters

Bitters are alcoholic infusions, too, but are unsweetened and flavored with bitter plant materials. Originally concocted as digestive aids, some bitters today are classified as unfit for use as beverages, and consequently are not subject to the same taxes and tariffs as other alcoholic beverages. Others are considered to be beverages. The former are used primarily as flavorings; the latter are drunk

ROOT BEER

Makes about 1 gallon

Root beer extracts, usually in an amount suitable for five gallons of beverage, are available commercially. These yield a drink that's very close in flavor to commercial root beers. Making your own infusions, however, allows for experimentation and a distinctive "house" brew. Ours is less sweet than most.

5 quarts water
1/4 ounce hops
1/2 ounce dried burdock root
1/2 ounce dried yellow dock root
1/2 ounce dried sarsaparilla root
1/2 ounce dried sassafras root
1/2 ounce dried spikenard root
1¹/₂ cups sugar
1/8 teaspoon granulated yeast

Simmer herbs in water for 30 minutes. Add sugar, stir to dissolve, and strain into a crock. Cool to lukewarm, add yeast, and stir well. Cover crock and leave to ferment for about an hour. Funnel into sterilized bottles (old beer or soft drink bottles will do), and cap tightly. Metal caps applied with a crimping tool, or wire-hinged caps are best. If you cork your bottles, tie or wire the corks down firmly and store bottles on their side to encourage sealing. Use only sturdy, returnable-type beer bottles or champagne bottles; those with twist-top caps are not strong enough.

---

before or after meals.

Among the flavoring bitters, Peychauds and Angostura bitters stand out. Peychauds is a flavoring agent for mixed drinks, and dashes of the 70-proof liquid are a required ingredient in many creole dishes. Angostura bitter includes gentian and other herbs and spices in a neutral spirit. This 90-proof spirit is dispensed in drops and dashes in Manhattans and Old Fashioneds as well as in cooking.

Averna bitter is flavored with herbs, aromatic roots, and caramel in a neutral grain spirit base, and is enjoyed "straight" along with espresso or mixed with soda and ice. Campari is probably the world's most popular bitter. The original formula of this bright red *aperitivo* includes herbs and fruits from four continents, blended and aged in oak barrels for a soft, sweet, yet pleasantly bitter flavor. Cynar bitter is made from artichokes and herbs in a brandy base. It is usually served on the rocks garnished with an orange slice.

Fernet Branca contains about 40 herbs and spices, including rhubarb, chamomile, saffron, cardamom, gentian, and myrrh in a neutral spirit base. Fernet translates as "hot iron", and refers to the poker-like tool used to heat the mixture of herbs and roots in the early years of its production. It's a favorite of Italians and Argentines as an aperitif. Germans prefer it with a beer chaser, and in other countries it's served with coffee after a meal.

Punt e Mes is a 33-proof bitter originally concocted by the addition of bitter quinine and other flavorings to vermouth (itself flavored with many herbs). Amer Picon contains, among other ingredients, gentian, cinchona bark (which yields quinine), and bitter orange in a brandy base. This 78-proof spirit is served on the rocks with soda at sidewalk cafes in Paris, sometimes sweetened with grenadine or cassis. Gammel Dansk is a dark, dry, peppery herbal brew, very popular in Denmark. Made from 20 herbs and some fruits in a spirit base, it is the most bitter of all bitters. Germans enjoy the spicy, bittersweet Jägermeister, one of the most easygoing of bitters, not unlike Chartreuse or Benedictine.

While liqueurs and bitters have been around a long time and are readily available at the grogshop, it's great fun to develop some of your own, using ingredients from your garden or pantry. Who knows—you may stumble onto a formula that will bring you fame and fortune! Be that as it may, we can assure you of great conversational bits as you serve your guests dishes or libations prepared from your own alchemy.

Creating your own homemade extracts, bitters, or liqueurs is easy. Just remember to use only potable alcohols (rubbing alcohol will *not* do) and garden products that are known to be edible. Extracts and bitters usually are not sweetened, but liqueurs usually are. You'll need glass containers, fresh or dried herbs, spices, and seeds, an 80- to 100-proof alcohol (rum, vodka, gin, brandy, or pure grain alcohol), and, if you like, citrus rinds.

As a rule, the formula is steeped from 4 to 6 weeks, then filtered and allowed to mature for a few more weeks. Decanted into sparkling bottles, antique or new, and garlanded with bright ribbons, they will make cherished gifts if you can bear to part with them.

A SIMPLE FRESH HERB LIQUEUR

This liqueur captures the flavor of fresh herb leaves, and is delicious with fruit or as a delicate aperitif.

1¹/₂ cups sugar
1/4 cup water
2 cups (firmly packed) leaves and tender stems of rose geranium, lemon balm, lemon verbena, or mint (red-stem apple mint recommended)
1 liter vodka

Combine sugar and water, bring to a boil, and stir until sugar is completely dissolved. Pack herbs in a large glass container. Cool syrup to lukewarm and pour over herbs, then add vodka. Cap and store in a cool, dark place at least one month, shaking occasionally. Strain and decant into bottles.

LOVAGE CORDIAL

Makes 1 pint

Cordials and wine made from lovage were popular in the eighteenth century. This lovage cordial is made with vodka, and is especially good in the Loving Mary Cocktail below. Use the hollow lovage stalk as a straw, or make a lovage umbrella for a fanciful garnish.

2 tablespoons fresh lovage seed
1 pint vodka
1/2 cup sugar
1 teaspoon coarsely ground black pepper
A few red pepper seeds

Crush the lovage seeds slightly and add the sugar, red and black pepper, and vodka in a one-quart glass jar. Stir well, seal, and place in a cool, dark place for at least 30 days. Strain and bottle.

LOVING MARY COCKTAIL

Serves 8 to 10

2 quarts fresh tomato juice
1/4 cup lemon juice
2 teaspoons Worcestershire sauce
1 tablespoon prepared horseradish
1 pint lovage cordial (above)

Combine all ingredients in a large glass pitcher and stir vigorously. Pour into tumblers over crushed ice. Garnish with lemon and fresh lovage stems with leaves or a lovage umbrella (see below).

LOVAGE "UMBRELLA"

To make an attractive garnish for drinks, cut a stalk of lovage the depth of your serving glass plus a few more inches. Cut thin slits about 1¹/₄ inch long all around the top of the stalk, then dip the stem in ice water; top slices will curl to form an umbrella.

A MASTER RECIPE FOR CORDIAL

Add a small amount of this cordial to meats, stews, or sauces, or serve as a digestive aperitif.

1/2 cup whole seeds of angelica, caraway, celery, cumin, coriander, dill, fennel, or combination
One or more of the following:
  2-inch stick cinnamon, 1 star anise, 1-inch piece mace blade, 4 allspice berries, 4 peppercorns, 4 cloves
Peel of 1 lemon, lime, or orange (colored portion only)
2 cups sugar
2 cups water
1 liter brandy or vodka

Bruise herb seeds and spices in a mortar or in a plastic bag with a rolling pin, then place them in a 2-quart glass container with spices and citrus peel. Combine sugar and water in a small saucepan and bring to a boil, stirring to dissolve sugar. Cool slightly, then pour syrup over seeds and spices. Add brandy or vodka and stir well to mix. Close and store in a cool, dark place for at least a month, shaking occasionally. Strain and decant into bottles.

THUNDER OF ZEUS

This makes an excellent aperitif and goes well with meats, poultry, sauces, fruit, and desserts (see White Chocolate and Pine Nut Mousse recipe on page 102). It's our very favorite formula.

1 liter very good brandy
2 tablespoons whole coriander seed
1 tablespoon whole cumin seed
6 whole cloves
1 2-inch piece cinnamon stick
2 cups sugar
2 cups water
1/2 vanilla bean, split
1 bottle very good dry white wine

Carefully warm the brandy to 115°F. Bruise the spices and seeds and add them to the hot liqueur. Pour into a bottle, seal, and store in a cool, dark place for at least a month.

When ready, dissolve sugar in water and add the

A lovage cordial is the basis of this Loving Mary Cocktail, recipe opposite.

vanilla bean. Add the aged brandy mixture and white wine, then rebottle, seal, and age for another month. Strain the liquid through cheesecloth or a coffee filter, pout it into bottles, and seal and store in a cool, dark place until used.

MAY WINE WITH STRAWBERRIES AND SWEET WOODRUFF

Makes about 3 quarts, or 24 servings

If the weather is hot and you plan on having the punch out for some time, it is important to have the ingredients well chilled.

1 handful (12 or more) sweet woodruff sprigs
3 pints fresh, ripe strawberries
1/2 cup sugar (or less if the berries are sweet)
2 bottles Rhine or Moselle wine
Sweet woodruff sprigs and blossoms for garnish
Edible flower blossoms for garnish (violets, johnny-jump-ups, pansies, or rose petals)
1 bottle champagne

Heat the handful of sweet woodruff sprigs on a baking sheet in a low oven for a few minutes to bring out the coumarin flavor. Rinse the berries lightly and pick them over, reserving 1 pint of the best for garnishing the punch.

Remove the stems from the 2 pints of berries, and add a pint of berries and half of the sugar to each of two pitchers. Crush the berries with the sugar (a potato masher works well), then add half the sweet woodruff and a bottle of wine to each pitcher and stir well. Cover the pitchers and refrigerate overnight or up to 24 hours.

Strain the wine to remove the fruit pulp and sweet woodruff, and pour the strained wine into a punch bowl. Stir in the champagne and garnish with whole strawberries, sweet woodruff sprigs, and flowers.

FESTIVE FRUIT DAIQUIRIS

4 to 6 servings

1 pound frozen unsweetened peaches (approximately 3 cups)
1 cup Bacardi dark rum
3 tablespoons fresh lemon juice
6–8 ice cubes
4–6 tablespoons herbal simple syrup (see below) made with lemony herbs
2 tablespoons freshly chopped lemony herbs, stems removed

Place frozen peaches in blender; add the rum and the ice cubes. Blend, adding the syrup to taste, along with the fresh herbs. Keep in freezer until serving time. Serve in long-stemmed glasses with a fresh peach slice and a sprig of lemon balm.

Variation: Use 2 tablespoons lime juice, Mexican marigold mint syrup, and 1 tablespoon freshly chopped Mexican marigold mint.

Strawberry Daiquiri: Use frozen unsweetened strawberries instead of peaches, syrup made with lemony herbs *or* a variety of mints, and garnish with fresh strawberries and a fresh herb sprig.

Pineapple Daiquiri: Use frozen unsweetened pineapple instead of peaches, syrup made with Mexican marigold mint *or* a variety of mints, and garnish with fresh pineapple and a fresh herb sprig.

Herbal Simple Syrup

2 cups white sugar
2 cups water
1½ cups tightly packed sweet herbs such as a combination of lemony herbs or a variety of mints or 1 cup Mexican marigold mint (which has a strong anise flavor)

Bring sugar and water to boil, stirring until sugar is dissolved. Reduce heat and add the fresh herbs; simmer 6 minutes. Allow to cool overnight; the syrup will take on a pretty golden or green tint, depending on which herbs you use. Strain into a sterilized bottle, and keep refrigerated to use as needed.

The sweetness of herbs

Serves 6 to 8

This dish makes an elegantly simple autumn or winter dessert.

6 to 8 firm, ripe pears (Bosc or Anjou are good)
3/4 to 1 bottle full-bodied red wine
1 cup port wine
2 or 3 pieces lemon peel
2 three-inch sprigs fresh rosemary
1/3 cup sugar

Peel the pears, leaving the stems on. Combine the rest of the ingredients in a stainless or enamel pan large enough to hold the pears in one layer. The pan should also be deep enough that the wine covers at least two-thirds of the pears when they are standing.

Bring the wine to a boil, then reduce to a simmer. Add the pears and poach them for about 25 minutes, turning them occasionally so they color evenly, until they are tender but firm. Remove them from the liquid and cool them on a platter. Remove the rosemary sprigs and boil the poaching liquid until it is reduced by half, then cool to room temperature.

10 to 12 ounces fresh chestnuts (or use canned chestnuts
*   packed in water)*
1 cup milk, or enough to barely cover
3-inch sprig fresh rosemary
3 tablespoons mild honey
1/2 pint whipping cream
Sugar

Slit the fresh chestnuts and put them in a noncorrodible saucepan. Cover them with about 2 inches of water and bring to a boil. Reduce heat and simmer for about 30 minutes. Drain and rinse the chestnuts. When they are cool enough to handle, remove their skins. If you're using canned chestnuts, just rinse and drain them.

Place the chestnuts in a small, noncorrodible saucepan with enough milk to barely cover them. Add the honey and rosemary and simmer for 10 to 15 minutes, then cool for about 15 minutes and remove the rosemary sprig.

Pass the chestnuts through the fine blade of a food mill or puree them in a food processor.

Whip the cream, adding a little sugar to taste, then fold the chestnut puree into the whipped cream. Refrigerate the cream until ready to assemble the dessert; remove about 10 minutes before serving time.

DESSERTS

To serve, stand the pears on individual dessert plates and drizzle them with the reduced poaching liquid. Spoon a generous dollop of chestnut cream alongside each pear and serve immediately.

NECTARINE AND PLUM CAKE WITH BERGAMOT

Makes a 9-by-13-inch cake

This is not a typical peach cake topped with fruit slices. Although the fruit is placed on top of the batter, the batter is so light that some of the fruit stays on top and some sinks to the bottom. This results in a very moist cake with fruit and herbs throughout.

You can make this cake with all nectarines or all plums, but the combination of the two fruits is superb. If you don't have bergamot leaves (*Monarda didyma*), use the same amount of orange mint leaves (*Mentha citrata*) for an equally delicious flavor.

3 medium-sized ripe nectarines
3 large plums, ripe but firm
1/4 cup sugar
2 to 3 tablespoons lemon juice
3 three-inch sprigs bergamot or orange mint

Peel the nectarines and plums. Slice the nectarines into twelfths and the plums into eighths and put them in a shallow bowl. Sprinkle the fruit slices with the sugar and lemon juice and toss with the herb sprigs, bruising the leaves against the side of the bowl to release their scent and flavor. Let the fruit and herbs stand, stirring them occasionally, while you prepare the cake batter.

14 tablespoons unsalted butter
5 extra-large eggs
2 extra-large egg yolks
1¹/₃ cups sugar
2 cups unbleached white flour
1/2 teaspoon salt
Finely grated zest of 1 lemon
About 20 bergamot or orange mint leaves (1/4 cup
   loosely packed leaves, finely shredded)

Butter and flour a 9- by-13-inch pan and preheat the oven to 375° F. Melt the butter over low heat and set aside to cool.

Beat the eggs, yolks, and sugar until the mixture becomes pale yellow, thick, and fluffy. This should take about 5 minutes.

Sift the flour with the salt three times. Gently fold the flour into the egg mixture, one-third at a time, then carefully fold the melted butter into the batter,

one-third at a time. When the batter is thoroughly blended, fold in the lemon zest.

Pour the batter into the prepared pan and spread it evenly, then strew the herbs over it. Arrange the fruit slices decoratively on top. (The leftover nectar is for the cook to sip after the cake is in the oven.)

Bake the cake for 40 minutes or until the edges of the cake are pale golden brown and pull away from the pan slightly, and a cake tester comes out clean. Do not overcook. Cool the cake in the pan on a baking rack.

The cake may be cut into squares and served from the pan, or the entire cake may be turned out onto a baking rack and then inverted and served from a platter. Serve it alone or accompanied by fresh whipped cream and garnished with a bergamot leaf or a few bergamot blossoms.

BAKED APPLES WITH SAVORY

Serves 6

This dish is finest in late summer with summer savory and Gravenstein apples, or early Winesaps, Empires, or McIntoshes, the warm baked apples garnished with flowering sprigs of savory and served with lightly whipped cream. But it's a tasty dish in winter or spring as well, as long as you have some fresh winter savory.

2/3 cup water
1/3 cup sugar
8 sprigs summer savory or 4 sprigs winter savory
5 tablespoons unsalted butter
1/3 cup walnuts or pecans
6 medium-sized apples, about 2¹/₂ pounds
Optional garnishes: 6 savory sprigs, whipped cream

Make a syrup by combining the water, sugar, and savory sprigs in a saucepan and simmering for about 10 minutes. Meanwhile, preheat the oven to 375° F. Melt 4 tablespoons of the butter; use the remaining tablespoon to butter a baking dish. Chop the nuts coarsely. Wash the apples and core them, being careful not to pierce the blossom ends. Cut out a little extra flesh from the apples as you remove the cores.

Remove the savory from the syrup, then mix the syrup and melted butter together. Divide the chopped nuts among the apples, filling the hollows loosely. Pour the syrup-butter mixture over the nuts. Bake for 30 minutes, or until apples are tender. Let them cool for 15 minutes or so before serving, or serve at room temperature. Garnish with savory sprigs, and pass whipped cream, if desired.

FRESH FRUIT TARTS WITH ORANGE MINT

Makes 18 tarts

These little tarts can be made with whatever fruit is in season, as long as it is perfectly ripe. If you like, two or more fruits can be combined to make a colorful array.

Pastry dough

1 3/4 cups unbleached white flour
2 pinches salt
1 1/2 tablespoons sugar
13 tablespoons unsalted butter (1 stick plus 5 tablespoons)
3 tablespoons cold water
1 egg white, lightly beaten, for glazing

Blend flour, salt, and sugar in a large bowl or a food processor. Cut the butter into 13 pieces, add it to the flour mixture, and cut it in with two knives, a pastry blender, or the food-processor blade until the mixture resembles coarse meal. Add water all at once and mix just until the mixture starts to come together. Do not overmix.

Turn the dough onto a pastry marble or board, gather it together, then flatten it into a disk. Wrap it in plastic and refrigerate it for at least 30 minutes. (At this point you can wrap it well and freeze it for up to 4 weeks.)

Use small tart pans or standard 2 1/2 -inch muffin tins to form these tarts. Pinch off small pieces of dough and press them into the tins to form the bottoms of the tart shells. Then pull off pieces and press the dough evenly against the sides. Press the dough just a bit above the rim of the pans, as it will slump a little during baking.

Cover the tart shells with plastic or foil and place in the freezer for at least 30 minutes. You can then bake them immediately or wrap them tightly and freeze them until you're ready to use them.

Preheat oven to 400° F. Bake the shells for 8 to 10 minutes or until pale golden brown. About halfway through baking, prick the bottoms with a fork if they are puffing up. Remove the tart shells from the oven and brush the insides very lightly with egg white and bake for another 2 minutes until just golden.

Cool the shells in the tins on baking racks until lukewarm. Gently remove them from the tins and finish cooling on baking racks. When completely cool, store in an airtight container until ready to fill.

Custard with Orange Mint

Bergamot or lemon balm can be used in making this custard, but orange mint (*Mentha citrata*) gives a delectable flavor with a hint of fragrance that goes especially well with summer fruits.

1 1/2 cups milk
4 or 5 three-inch sprigs orange mint
1/3 cup sugar
1 tablespoon and 1 teaspoon cornstarch
Pinch salt
3 extra-large egg yolks
1/4 teaspoon pure vanilla extract

Scald the milk with the orange mint, bruising the sprigs against the side of the pan with the back of a wooden spoon. Steep for 30 to 60 minutes or until the milk has cooled. Remove the herb sprigs, squeezing them to extract their flavor.

Combine the sugar, cornstarch, and salt in a separate bowl, then add them to the milk. Place the pan over medium heat and whisk the ingredients well. Beat the egg yolks lightly. When the milk mixture starts to get hot, add about 1/3 cup of it to the egg yolks and whisk well, then pour the egg mixture into the pan and whisk well. Continue cooking and whisking as the mixture thickens. When the first bubble appears in the custard, start timing 30 seconds, stirring constantly. Remove from heat when time is up.

Pour the custard into a bowl to cool, whisking every 5 minutes or so to release the steam. When the custard is lukewarm, stir in the vanilla, cover with waxed paper, and chill. (The custard can be made a day ahead.)

Assembling the tarts

About 1/2 cup red currant jelly or 1 cup apricot preserves
4 or 5 small apricots or plums or 3 small peaches or
* 1 pint berries*

Melt the jelly or preserves in a small saucepan over low heat. Strain preserves to remove large pieces of pulp. Peel apricots, plums, or peaches. Slice thinly any fruits larger than medium berry size; rinse berries and pick over.

Spoon a heaping tablespoon of custard into each tart shell and arrange fruit slices or berries on top. Brush the melted jelly or preserves over the fruit. These are best assembled at the last minute, but they can be prepared up to 2 hours in advance. Keep the prepared tarts cool.

Sweet Thyme Vinegar Pie

Serves 6 to 8

This recipe is adapted from an old standard that's often—and somewhat nostalgically—requested in the food pages of modern newspapers.

1/2 cup softened butter or margarine
1¼ cups sugar
2 tablespoons lemon thyme vinegar
3 eggs, beaten
1 teaspoon vanilla
1/3 cup raisins or currants
1/3 cup broken pecans, walnuts, or shredded coconut
1 eight-inch pie shell, unbaked
Lemon thyme sprigs, with flowers if possible, for garnish

Cream together the butter and sugar until light and fluffy. Add vinegar, eggs, and vanilla, and beat well. Sprinkle raisins and nuts evenly in pie shell. Carefully pour butter and egg mixture over the raisins and nuts, then bake at 350° F for 45 minutes or until a knife blade inserted in the center comes out clean. Cool on a rack. Garnish with lemon thyme sprigs; serve warm or at room temperature.

Variation: Separate eggs and reserve whites to make a meringue with 3 tablespoons sugar beaten in. Bake filling as above, cool, then top with meringue and bake 6 to 8 minutes more to brown.

Herbal Crepe with Strawberries and Bananas

Serves 6

Crepe:
3 eggs, beaten
1½ cups unbleached all-purpose flour
1½ cups milk
1/4 teaspoon salt
1/4 teaspoon white pepper
1/4 cup plus 2 tablespoons melted butter
1/4 cup sage, basil, mint, or tarragon, minced

Filling:
2 bananas, peeled and sliced
1 cup slivered strawberries
1 cup low-fat vanilla yogurt
1 cup granola
1/4 teaspoon cinnamon

For the crepe, use a whisk to combine the eggs, flour, milk, salt, and pepper in a large mixing bowl. Whisk in the butter and herbs and refrigerate for 15 to 30 minutes.

Lightly oil a 9-inch crepe pan or nonstick skillet. Preheat as for pancakes; don't let the oil smoke. Ladle in about 1/2 cup batter, and tilt the pan to spread the batter into a thin, round crepe. When the edges of the crepe are light brown, flip it with a smooth motion. Continue cooking until the second side is light brown, then remove to a warm plate. Cook the remaining batter in the same fashion.

For the filling, toss the bananas, strawberries, yogurt, granola, and cinnamon in a mixing bowl. Fill each crepe with about 1/2 cup of the fruit mixture, forming a log in the middle and wrapping the crepe around the filling (like a burrito). Serve immediately.

Brandy Madeleines

Makes 18 cakes

These are not the madeleines that Proust remembered at such loving length; these are based on a sponge cake batter, and are light and buttery—just right with a tea brewed with lemongrass or lemon verbena.

4 large eggs at room temperature
2/3 cup sugar
2 teaspoons vanilla
1 tablespoon brandy
3/4 cup unsalted butter, melted and cooled to room temperature
2/3 cup sifted all-purpose flour, sifted together with
1/3 cup sifted cake flour

Grease and flour a madeleine tile or tiny muffin tins, and preheat oven to 375° F. Beat eggs, sugar, vanilla, and brandy together until very light and fluffy and all sugar is dissolved. Add about half the flour mixture and fold in lightly. Add cooled butter and remaining flour alternately, working quickly and stirring batter as little as possible. Fill tins half full and bake for 10–12 minutes, or until cakes are golden and come out of the tins easily.

Double Ginger Pumpkin Pie

Disguised as an ordinary, run-of-the-mill pumpkin pie, this version has a crunchy surprise layer in the bottom that helps keep the crust from becoming soggy. The filling can be made from home-grown pumpkin—a messy and tedious process. You can emulate the flavor and texture with canned pumpkin, though, if you take time to caramelize it lightly by stirring it over medium-high heat in a heavy skillet for half an hour or so.

Sweet Thyme Vinegar Pie, recipe opposite.

1 unbaked 9-inch single crust pie shell, well-pricked with
  a fork
2 tablespoons brown sugar
2 tablespoons softened butter
4 tablespoons finely chopped crystallized ginger
4 tablespoons finely chopped walnuts
2 large eggs
1/2 cup brown sugar
1 16-ounce can unseasoned pumpkin
1 teaspoon ground ginger
1/2 teaspoon ground cinnamon
1/2 teaspoon ground allspice
1 cup light cream
Lightly sweetened whipped cream for garnish

Preheat the oven to 400° F. Combine the 2 table-spoons of sugar, butter, crystallized ginger, and walnuts until crumbly. Gently press mixture into the bottom of the pie shell. Bake in the preheated oven until bubbly and golden brown, about 10 minutes.

While crust is baking, whisk eggs with 1/2 cup brown sugar, pumpkin, spices, and cream until smooth. Pour filling into the prebaked shell and bake until a table knife inserted toward the edge just comes out clean, about 40 minutes. (The center should be moist, since it continues cooking as it cools.) Cool pie on a wire rack and serve in wedges with whipped cream.

STRAWBERRY RHUBARB COBBLER

Serves 6

Sweet woodruff doesn't have much of an aroma when picked fresh, but when dried or cooked, it imparts a homey flavor, rather like adding a taste of vanilla and a scent of fresh-mown hay. Serve this dessert with vanilla ice cream or fresh whipped cream, garnished with a fresh sprig of sweet woodruff.

4 cups rhubarb, cut into 1/2-inch dice
4 cups fresh strawberries, halved
About 1 cup sugar
10 or 12 fresh 3-inch sprigs sweet woodruff
2¹/₂ tablespoons unbleached flour

Place rhubarb, berries, sugar, and sweet woodruff in a saucepan, toss well, and bring to a simmer over medium high heat, stirring the fruit as it releases its juices. Reduce heat, stir, and cook for 3 to 5 minutes. Remove from heat and set aside. Let the mixture cool a bit and remove the woodruff sprigs, then stir the flour into the fruit.

1¹/₃ cups unbleached flour
2¹/₂ tablespoons sugar
1/2 teaspoon salt
2 teaspoons baking powder
6 tablespoons cold unsalted butter, cut into pieces
1 cup milk

Preheat oven to 425° F and butter a 2¹/₂-quart baking dish.

Combine the flour, sugar, salt, and baking powder in a bowl. Cut the butter into the flour mixture until it is in pea-sized lumps. Add the milk to the flour mixture and mix with a fork until just blended.

Transfer the fruit to the buttered baking dish, and drop the dough in large spoonfuls over it. Bake the cobbler for 15 minutes, then reduce heat to 350° F. Bake for 15 to 20 minutes more, or until the fruit is bubbling and the dough is turning golden brown. Serve warm or at room temperature.

CHEESE THUMBPRINTS

Makes about 30 cookies

These little pastries are not too sweet, so the herb flavor shines. They're even better the second day.

2 cups flour
1 tablespoon herb honey
3/4 cup butter, softened
3-ounce package cream cheese
1/2 teaspoon salt
1/4 teaspoon baking powder
Herb honey jelly for filling (see page 110)
Powdered sugar

Mix all ingredients together. Roll 1/2 inch thick. Cut with a round 1¹/₂-inch cookie cutter that has a crimped edge. Press a dent in the center of each cookie with your thumb and fill with 1/4 to 1/2 teaspoon of herb honey jelly (rose geranium, lemon verbena, and lavender are nice). Bake at 350° F for 20 to 25 minutes or until pastries just begin to brown. Sprinkle with powdered sugar.

LEMON BALM
POPPY SEED TEA LOAVES

This is a lovely lemon-scented cake, not too sweet. You may substitute lemon verbena for the balm. The recipe makes two 9-by-5-inch loaves or six 6-by-3-inch loaves; because they smell so good when they are baking, you might want to make one large loaf to eat right away and three small ones to give away.

1 cup milk
4 three-inch sprigs fresh lemon balm or 1 small handful
 dried lemon balm leaves
1 cup unsalted butter, at room temperature
1½ cups sugar
6 eggs, separated, at room temperature
Grated zest of 2 lemons
3 cups unbleached flour
1½ teaspoons baking powder
1/4 teaspoon salt
1/2 cup poppy seed

Combine the milk and balm in a small saucepan, bruising the fresh sprigs against the side of the pan with a spoon. Scald the milk and remove from heat.

Butter the pans and flour them lightly. Preheat the oven to 350° F.

In a large bowl, cream the butter, gradually beat in the sugar, and beat until light and fluffy. Add the egg yolks, one at a time, beating well after each addition. Stir in the lemon zest.

Sift the dry ingredients together. Remove the balm from the milk and discard. Add the flour mixture to the batter, a third at a time, alternating with the milk, stirring well by hand after each addition. Fold the poppy seeds in with the last third of the flour.

Beat the egg whites until stiff. Fold about a third of the whites into the batter, then gently fold in the remaining whites. Spoon the batter into the prepared pans, filling them a little more than halfway. Bake the loaves until they are just turning golden brown and a tester comes out clean; small loaves take about 30 minutes, and large loaves take about 45 minutes.

Lemon Syrup

1/3 cup sugar
1/4 cup water
3 tablespoons fresh lemon juice
5 3-inch sprigs lemon balm or 1/4 cup loosely packed
 dried balm leaves

While the loaves are baking, prepare the syrup. Combine all the ingredients in a small saucepan, and cook over medium heat, stirring until the syrup comes to a boil. Remove from heat.

Cool the loaves in the pans for about 10 minutes. Remove the herb leaves from the syrup, and brush the loaves with it. Use all the syrup, dividing it evenly among the loaves. Turn loaves out on cooling rack and cool completely.

Wrap loaves well in heavy plastic wrap or foil. They will keep for 4 or 5 days at cool room temperature

or about a week in the refrigerator, or they can be frozen for several months.

CORIANDER TEA TORTE

Serves 8

This European-style dessert is full of flavor and interestingly delicious. It is only about 1 to 1½ inches tall and a bit more dry and dense than cakelike. Prunes are preferred, and they should be moist and sticky; if they are dry and leathery, soak them in warm water for 20 to 30 minutes and drain them well. Dried apricots, treated in the same way, can be substituted.

3/4 cup granulated sugar
1¼ cups unbleached flour
1/2 teaspoon salt
1 teaspoon baking powder
1 tablespoon and 2 teaspoons coriander seed,
 toasted and ground
Zest of 1 lemon
1/2 cup cold unsalted butter, cut into 8 pieces
2 extra-large eggs
1/2 teaspoon pure vanilla extract
1 cup sliced pitted prunes, cut into strips
2 teaspoons confectioners' sugar

Lightly grease and flour a 9- or 9½-inch tart or springform pan with a removable bottom. Preheat the oven to 350° F.

In a bowl (or food processor), combine the granulated sugar, flour, salt, baking powder, 1 tablespoon of ground coriander seed, and lemon zest and blend well. Add the butter and cut it (or pulse) until the mixture is a coarse meal. Add the eggs and vanilla and stir (or process) until the dough just comes together.

Transfer the batter to the prepared pan, spreading it evenly with a spatula. Arrange the prune slivers decoratively on the batter, pressing them lightly.

Bake the torte in the center of the oven for 25 to 30 minutes, until golden brown on top or a cake tester comes out clean. Cool on a baking rack while still in the pan.

Mix the remaining ground coriander with the confectioners' sugar. After the torte has cooled for 10 minutes, sift the spiced sugar over the top of the cake. Let cool, remove the tart ring, and serve at room temperature. This torte is lovely served with tea, or with fresh fruit for dessert.

HOLIDAY SEED CAKE

3 cups sifted all-purpose flour
2 1/2 teaspoons baking powder
1 teaspoon ground mace
1 teaspoon ground cardamom seed
1 teaspoon salt
2/3 cup butter or margarine
2 cups granulated sugar
4 eggs
3 tablespoons finely chopped lemon rind (yellow part only)
1 cup milk
1 tablespoon caraway seeds
1 tablespoon poppy seeds
1 teaspoon aniseed
Powdered sugar

Grease and flour a 10-inch tube or bundt pan. Preheat oven to 350° F. Sift together the flour, baking powder, mace, cardamom, and salt; set aside. In a large bowl, cream butter and sugar until light and fluffy. Add eggs one at a time, beating well after each addition. Blend in lemon rind.

Gradually add sifted dry ingredients to butter mixture, alternating with milk, in 4 to 6 increments. Stir in seeds, making sure all dry ingredients are evenly combined.

Pour batter into prepared pan, smoothing top evenly. Bake about 1 hour, or until cake begins to pull away from sides of pan and a cake tester comes out dry. If cake begins to brown too soon, cover lightly with a piece of foil. Remove cake from oven and let cool about 15 minutes on a rack before turning out. Sprinkle with powdered sugar, sifting it through a doily to produce a decorative pattern if you wish. Serve warm with Classic Lemon Curd.

CLASSIC LEMON CURD

2 whole eggs
2 egg yolks
1 cup sugar
2/3 cup fresh lemon juice
1 cup butter

For a fast, updated method of making this classic sauce, place all ingredients in blender or processor; mix till smooth. Pour into a stainless or ceramic double boiler; cook over simmering water until thick, stirring constantly. If you are very careful, you can cook sauce over direct heat. Be sure to use a heavy-bottomed pan, and stir constantly in a figure eight, making sure to scrape the edges well.

Serve sauce warm over cake, ice cream, or puddings. Store leftovers in refrigerator and warm before serving.

WHITE CHOCOLATE AND PINE NUT MOUSSE

Serves 8–10

This delicate, creamy white dessert is attractive any way you serve it; the rose geranium garnish sets off the colors of the mousse and sauce particularly well.

Mousse

8 ounces white chocolate, chopped in 1/2-inch pieces or grated
1 tablespoon unflavored gelatin
2 1/2 cups heavy cream
1/2 cup rose geranium leaves
Peel of 1 orange
6 egg yolks
2 tablespoons Thunder of Zeus (page 92) or other liqueur
2 egg whites
1 tablespoon sugar
1/2 cup toasted pine nuts, chopped fine (or substitute hazelnuts or almonds)
Mocha Chocolate Sauce (optional, below)
Fresh fruit, rose geranium flowers, and extra pine nuts for garnish (optional)

Blend chocolate pieces and salt in food processor bowl with steel knife for 30 seconds. Combine 1/4 cup cream with the gelatin and set aside. Combine 1 1/4 cups cream with geranium leaves and orange peel, bring to a boil, then reduce heat and simmer 5 minutes. Add dissolved gelatin and simmer 2 to 3 minutes more. Strain, pressing on leaves and peel to extract all liquids. Add hot cream mixture to pulverized chocolate and process about 15 seconds. Add egg yolks and liqueur and process 10 seconds more. Pour mixture into a large mixing bowl and refrigerate until cool but not firm.

Beat egg whites until soft peaks form. Gradually add 1 tablespoon sugar and continue beating until stiff peaks form. Beat about 1/3 of the whipped egg whites into the cooled chocolate mixture to lighten. With a rubber spatula, gently fold in remaining beaten egg whites. Whip remaining 1 cup cream and fold into mixture along with toasted pine nuts. Chill several hours before serving. Mousse may be piped through a pastry tube into serving dish or individual dishes. If desired, top with Mocha Chocolate Sauce, and garnish with fruit, rose geraniums, or pine nuts.

Holiday Seed Cake with Lemon Curd, recipe opposite.

Mocha Chocolate Sauce

12 ounces semisweet chocolate
3 to 4 tablespoons cream
2 tablespoons Thunder of Zeus (page 92) or other liqueur
1 to 2 tablespoons instant espresso dissolved in cream
(optional)

Melt chocolate in double boiler over simmering water or in microwave oven for 2 minutes at full power, stirring once while melting. Thin with cream and liqueur. Add espresso if desired. Serve warm.

CINNAMON BASIL CUSTARD

Serves 4

The subtle flavor of Cinnamon basil is a refreshing alternative to the usual spice.

4 cups milk
1 cup cinnamon basil leaves
4 eggs
1/2 cup sugar

Bring milk to scalding point in a saucepan over medium heat. Skim off the top and submerge basil leaves in the hot milk. Cover the pan and allow the basil to steep for 20 minutes.

Meanwhile, preheat the oven to 350° F. In a bowl, beat the eggs with the sugar. Strain out the basil leaves and slowly reheat the milk. Stir the milk into the eggs and sugar. Pour into a 1-quart baking dish or individual custard cups. Place the dish or cups in a pan of hot water; the water should be level with the custard. Bake for 45 minutes, or test by inserting a clean knife into the center of the custard. If the knife comes out clean, the custard is done. Cool dish or cups on a wire rack. Serve the custard at room temperature or chilled.

CHOCOLATE STRAWBERRY TOSTADAS

Serves 6

Strawberry Sauce

1¹/₂ cups sliced fresh strawberries
1/3 cup strawberry jam (without sugar, if available)
1 tablespoon Tia Maria, or liqueur of your choice

Place sliced strawberries, jam, and liqueur in a blender or food processor and puree until well blended. Refrigerate until serving time (can be made a day ahead).

Tostadas

1/4 flour
2 tablespoons cocoa powder
3¹/₂ tablespoons sugar
1/2 teaspoon baking powder
1 tablespoon + 1 teaspoon vegetable shortening
3 tablespoons cold water

Sift dry ingredients and cut in shortening until coarse (may be done in a food processor). Add water and stir until blended. Knead for 30 seconds. Cover and let set for 30 minutes. Shape into 6 rounds, cover, and let set for 30 minutes. Roll in 4-inch circles on floured board and fit into muffin cups that have been coated with cooking spray. Fold excess dough outward to make an edge. Bake for 10 minutes at 350° F.

Filling

1/4 teaspoon nutmeg
1/2 teaspoon cinnamon
1/2 teaspoon allspice
3 cups (2 pints) vanilla frozen yogurt or ice milk
6 whole strawberries, for garnish
6 fresh mint sprigs, for garnish

Combine nutmeg, cinnamon, and allspice. Soften frozen yogurt and swirl the spice mixture through it. Refreeze until serving time. Set a "tostada" on each plate, spoon the strawberry sauce around them, fill each with one-sixth of the frozen yogurt, and garnish with the additional strawberries and mint leaves. Serve immediately.

DESSERTS

Herbal Sorbet—
Simple, Delicious Ways to Cool Down

Appetizer, side dish, salad dressing, palate refresher, summer cooler, dessert—sorbet is not only surprisingly easy to make but is one of the most versatile of frozen treats. And when fresh or dried herbs are added, their flavors really stand out.

Sorbet is not just the French word for sherbet; it differs from sherbet in that it contains no milk, egg white, or gelatin. During formal Victorian dinners, which could last two or three hours, as many as three of the courses were likely to be some kind of sorbet. Most were basically lemon sorbet with other flavorings added, a fine trick you can use today to invent herbal flavors of your own.

HERBAL SORBET BASICS

For the smoothest-textured sorbet, start with a simple syrup made by boiling sugar and water together—at least one cup of sugar per quart of water—for up to five minutes. Remove the syrup from the heat and cool it to room temperature. You can add herbs immediately after boiling so they steep while the syrup cools, or you can puree them separately with a portion of the sugar, combine the puree with the cooled syrup, and let the mixture stand for at least an hour before straining out the herbs. (The latter method is recommended for herbs whose delicate or complex flavors may be obliterated by heat.)

Alternatively, you can simply puree the herbs with a portion of the sugar, dissolve the remaining sugar in the water, and add the puree. Set the mixture aside for at least an hour, then strain out the herbs. Keep in mind, though, that boiling the syrup (or at least part of the syrup) makes a smoother sorbet. If time is a factor, the pan of syrup can be cooled in ice water after boiling.

SWEETENING

Although a sorbet is supposed to be tart, its puckering quality is offset by sweetness, and the kind of sweetener you choose will affect the texture of the sorbet. Cane sugar gives sorbet its characteristic texture, preventing it from becoming too coarse or freezing too firmly. Excessive sugar can keep the sorbet from freezing at all; but that much sugar would be unpleasant to taste.

Many people who prefer the cold method rather than boiling use fructose instead of cane sugar. This fruit-derived sugar dissolves readily without heating. The resulting sorbet, however, isn't nearly as smooth as a sorbet based on boiled sugar syrup. Honey can be used in sorbet if you reduce the amount of liquid slightly, but its flavor is overwhelming. It can work well in a strong lemon sorbet, but we don't otherwise recommend sweetening with honey unless what you want is honey-flavored sorbet. Corn syrup, substituted for up to 1/3 the sugar and with a slight reduction in liquid, helps prevent crystallization on the surface of the sorbet during storage. It also raises the melting point of the sorbet so it feels less cold in your mouth. Sweetener that is more than 1/3 corn syrup, however, can cause the sorbet to freeze too hard.

You can make sugar-free sorbet by substituting a nonnutritive sweetener (such as saccharin or aspartame) for sugar. If you use these, check the manufacturer's instructions about how to substitute the sweetener for sugar and how it reacts to heat. (Some lose and some gain sweetness when heated.) Alternatively, you can steep the herbs in naturally sweet apple juice, apple juice concentrate, or pineapple juice, and omit additional sweetener. Boiling will not be necessary.

FLAVORING

For each quart of sorbet you'll need about 1/2 cup of fresh or 1/4 cup dried herbs. You can vary these amounts to suit your taste and the flavor intensity of the herbs you use.

The most popular individual herbs for sorbet are mint, lavender, rosemary, and scented geranium, but feel free to experiment with your favorites. Tarragon, purple sage, and sweet cicely also go quite nicely in sorbet. You can combine herbs to create your own signature sorbet; any herbs you use in tea should make a palatable sorbet.

You can make the sugar syrup with your favorite tea instead of water. Brew the tea at least twice as strong as usual, and include something tart, such as a pinch of dried, ground rose hips, or add lemon juice just before freezing the sorbet. (Rose hips not only increase a sorbet's depth of flavor, but also tint it a pretty pink.) However, the herb flavor will be stronger if you use either rose hip or lemon sorbet as your base and flavor it with fresh or dried herbs. Lemon-based sorbet has little color of its own; herbs sometimes give it a greenish tint.

For a really different and tasty sorbet to serve as an appetizer or palate cleanser, use tomato juice as your base. Flavor the sorbet (either by heating the tomato juice or using the cold method) with basil, dill, oregano, or parsley, or your favorite spaghetti-sauce herb blend. Added sweetener is optional. This mix can be spiced up with a touch of Tabasco or a dash of Worcestershire.

Freezing

The softest, finest-textured sorbets are made in an ice cream maker. After the herbs have been strained out, refrigerate the mix for several hours or overnight before freezing. This aging not only makes a smoother sorbet, but it ensures that the ice cream machine will not be overworked or fail to freeze the sorbet.

A sorbet needs room to expand as it aerates and freezes, so fill the canister only about two-thirds to three-quarters full, or to the fill line. The recipes below yield one quart of sorbet; if your machine has a smaller capacity, either divide the recipe and make a smaller amount or freeze the mix in more than one batch. If in doubt, follow the manufacturer's instructions. The recipes can be doubled or divided without any additional adjustments.

If you don't have or prefer not to use an ice cream maker, you can (at the expense of fine texture) freeze sorbet in your household freezer. One simple way is to freeze the mix as cubes and whirl them in a food processor at serving time; the result will be similar to granita (see below). However, you run the risk of getting unpleasant lumps or, worse, having the sorbet melt down too much because of the heat of the blender, while guests wait expectantly at the table.

Proper sorbet has the approximate consistency of densely packed snow. No matter what sweetener is used, the sorbet's texture and flavor will be best at soft-serve consistency. Stored in a freezer for more than one to three days, many sorbets (and all sugar-free ones) become either too firm or too crumbly to scoop, and a fully frozen sorbet doesn't impart its finest flavor.

If time constraints require making a sorbet in advance and holding it in the freezer until serving time, you can temper it to scooping consistency by setting it in the refrigerator for 20 to 30 minutes. Another strategy, if the room isn't too warm, is to heap the sorbet into hollowed-out fruit or vegetable shells garnished with sprigs of fresh herbs to create an attractive centerpiece where the sorbet can soften while your meal progresses.

Granita

Another alternative is to turn your sorbet mix into a granita. Compared to a sorbet, which is stir-frozen (beaten while freezing takes place), a granita is still-frozen (frozen without constant beating). As a result, less air is incorporated, and the granita has a stronger flavor than the sorbet.

The word "granita" comes from the Italian word for "grainy", which aptly describes the coarse texture that results from still freezing. Traditionally, granita is grated or shaved, making it incredibly light and powdery. Sometimes it's chipped, instead, into icy shards.

Homemade granita, which looks remarkably like sparkling edible sequins, is made by freezing the mix in trays and periodically raking it with a fork. The idea is to break apart the developing ice crystals without destroying their characteristic shape.

For the sake of convenience, the mix may be prepared a day in advance and refrigerated in a covered container. A few hours before serving, stir the mix well, pour it into shallow freezer trays, and place them in your freezer. If possible, adjust the freezer to its lowest setting. With a fork, gently crush the icy lumps two or three times as freezing progresses. Depending on the efficiency of your freezer, the granita will be ready to serve in two to three hours.

Just before serving, lighten the texture by raking the granita once more with a fork. To slow melting, serve it in prechilled bowls or glasses. Tuck in a fresh herbal sprig of mixed or matched flavor.

HERBED LEMON SORBET

Fresh lemons give the best flavor to this basic sorbet. You can scrape out the shells and use them as sorbet serving dishes.

1¹/₃ cups sugar
2²/₃ cups water
1/4 cup dried or 1/2 cup fresh herbs, crushed
1¹/₃ cups lemon juice (juice of 6 or 7 lemons)

In a saucepan, bring the sugar and water to a boil and simmer up to 5 minutes (or microwave in a non-metal container on high for up to 3 minutes). Remove from heat, add the herbs, and cool to room temperature. Strain, then stir in the lemon juice. Cover and chill for 1 to 2 hours.

Freeze the mix in an ice cream maker according to the manufacturer's directions, or place it in shallow trays in your household freezer and rake periodically with a fork.

Garnish each serving with a twist of lemon and an herb sprig.

BASIC ROSE HIP SORBET

This rather plain-tasting sorbet makes a terrific base for herbal flavors and contributes a delightful pink color. Simply substitute herbs for a portion of the rose hips. To make pink mint sorbet, for example, substitute 3 tablespoons of crushed dried mint (or 6 tablespoons fresh mint) for an equal amount of rose hips. You can also flavor the basic mix with a small amount of a blend of spices such as allspice, cinnamon, and cloves. Or use a blended rose hip tea instead of plain rose hips (three tea bags equal about one tablespoon).

1¹/₃ cups sugar
4 cups water
4 tablespoons dried or 1/2 cup fresh rose hips, crushed

In a saucepan, bring the sugar and water to a boil and simmer 5 minutes (or microwave in nonmetal container on high for up to 3 minutes). Remove from heat, stir in the rose hips, and cool to room temperature. Strain. Cover and chill 1 to 2 hours.

Freeze in an ice cream maker according to the manufacturer's directions or place in shallow trays in your household freezer and rake periodically with a fork.

CANTALOUPE SORBET

Makes about 1 quart

This sorbet makes a refreshing summertime dessert, no matter which herb you choose to add to it. When made with lemon balm, it has a hint of lemon and seems slightly sweeter; pineapple sage imparts a more subtle and herby flavor; and it surprises the palate with spiciness when made with lemon basil.

1/4 cup sugar
1 cup boiling water
10 to 12 leaves lemon balm or pineapple sage,
  2¹/₂ to 3 inches long
1 medium cantaloupe
1 cup chilled Asti Spumante
Lemon balm or pineapple sage leaves for garnish

In a small saucepan, dissolve the sugar in the water with the herb leaves. Bring the syrup to a simmer and cook for a few minutes. Remove from heat and let cool to room temperature.

Remove the seeds from the melon and cut the pulp into chunks; there should be 3¹/₂ to 4 cups pulp. Remove the herb leaves from the syrup.

In a food processor or blender, puree the melon with the syrup in batches until smooth. Pour the melon puree into the canister of an ice cream maker, then stir in the Asti Spumante. Freeze the sorbet according to manufacturer's instructions. Serve garnished with herb leaves or blossoms.

VIOLET ICE CREAM

Whip 1 cup of heavy cream until stiff. Fold in 2 cups of fine, fresh whole wheat bread crumbs (about four medium slices) and 1/4 cup crystallized raw (turbinado) sugar. Chill in the freezer until stiff but not hard.

Before serving, mix in a few crystallized violets, and garnish each serving with more of the same.

Gifts & condiments

Flavored Vinegars

One of the easiest and prettiest ways to store up summer's flavors is by making herbed vinegars. Put a handful of clean, fresh, coarsely torn herbs in a quart jar. Fill the jar with a mild vinegar (wine, cider, or distilled), and set in a warm, sunny spot for two or three weeks. Some herbs impart color to white vinegars; chive blossoms yield a delicate pink, opal basil a rich ruby, tarragon a pale gold.

Strain vinegar into fresh bottles and discard the now-limp and colorless herbs. Add a fresh sprig to each bottle for identification, if you wish. Use your flavored vinegar in salad dressings, sauces, and marinades, or as a condiment.

Some herbs for vinegar: tarragon; basil—green and purple; borage—leaves and flowers; chives—chive blossoms, garlic chives; salad burnet; garlic—use five or six cloves per quart; mint; dill.

Try combinations of herbs: basil/garlic, oregano/thyme, whatever herbs you enjoy together fresh. You

FOUR THIEVES VINEGAR

The legends surrounding this formula are numerous. It originally included dozens of herbs and spices (some quite surprising) and supposedly was used by the nomadic Bedouins to marinate tough lamb, preserve its freshness in hot climates, and cover the tainted taste of old meats. This vinegar can be strained if desired and repacked with fresh herb sprigs and seasonings. It is excellent with red meats and for game marinades, pickled beets and eggs, and salad dressings.

16 ounces red wine vinegar
1 teaspoon whole cloves
1 three-inch stick cinnamon
1 teaspoon each black peppercorns, whole allspice, whole
*   mustard seed, whole fennel seed*
1/2 teaspoon salt
1 large clove garlic
1 sprig fresh rue
3–4 sprigs fresh sage
4–6 sprigs each fresh spearmint, rosemary, and tarragon
6–8 stems salad burnet

Warm the vinegar *just slightly* with spices, seeds, and salt. Stir to make sure salt is dissolved. Let the mixture cool to room temperature, then pour it over the herbs. Let stand at least three days to blend flavors.

can make lovely raspberry or blueberry vinegars in the same way, discarding the spent fruit after several weeks of soaking.

SUGGESTED COMBINATIONS

Mediterranean Sea. Red wine or cider vinegar. Garlic, bay, chile, rosemary, sage, thyme, mild oregano, lavender flowers, parsley, fennel seed, and orange peel.

Pacific Rim. Rice wine vinegar. Garlic, Thai chile or Szechuan peppers, fresh or dry ginger or galangal root, melegueta peppers, lemongrass, coriander (regular, thorny, or Vietnamese type), spearmint, cinnamon basil, garlic chives, and star anise.

Sweet Herb and Flower. White wine, rice wine, fruit, or cider vinegar. Marigold, nasturtiums, red or pink dianthus, chive blossoms, flowers of purple, cinnamon, or lemon basil, lemon verbena, lemon balm, mints, rose or lemon geranium, mint marigold (*Tagetes lucida*), and a small amount of rosemary or sage.

Dilly Lemon Thyme. White wine or rice wine vinegar. Dill seed, dill leaf, garlic, lemon thyme, lemon balm, lemon basil, bay leaf, and lemon peel.

Hearty Bouquet. Red wine or cider vinegar. Shallot, garlic, bay leaf, thyme, marjoram, sage, winter savory, parsley, coriander seed, whole cloves (1 tablespoon per pint), cinnamon stick (3-inch piece per pint), and white or black peppercorns.

Marinade for Game and Red Meats. Red or white wine, fruit, or cider vinegar. Shallots, garlic, juniper berries (1 tablespoon per pint), bay leaf, chiles, thyme, sage, parsley, allspice, cloves, black peppercorns, coriander seed, caraway seed, cumin seed, and melegueta peppers.

Delicate Salad. White or rice wine, fruit, or cider vinegar. Chives (and chive blossoms), marigolds, nasturtiums, salad burnet, parsley, tarragon, mint marigold, spearmint, lemon balm, and basil (leaves and flowers).

LEMONY CHILE VINEGAR

The amounts of material added to this vinegar are not critical; just be sure to use plenty.

16 ounces white wine vinegar
Peel of 1 lemon and 1 lime
1/2 cup lemon thyme sprigs
1 handful garlic or onion chives
2–3 cloves garlic, peeled and cut in half
3–4 small dried red chiles
1 tablespoon whole coriander seed
1 tablespoon whole cumin seed
4 to 6 bay leaves, fresh or dry

Cover seasonings with vinegar at room temperature. Seal with a glass stopper or plastic-lined lid. Store in a cool, dark place for at least 2 days before using. Strain if desired and pack with a fresh piece of lemon peel and lemon thyme.

FRESH HERBAL OIL CONCENTRATE

Reach for a fresh herbal oil concentrate instead of fresh or dried herbs. When substituting for fresh herbs, use about 1/3 the amount called for. Great for sauces, soups, salad dressings, basting mixtures, and vegetable salads, and in sour cream or yogurt for quick sauces or dips.

2 hard-packed cups herb leaves and tender stems, single or combination (parsley may be added if needed to make measurement), or fresh, peeled cloves of garlic
1/2 cup good-quality vegetable oil (We do not recommend olive oil because it has a distinct taste of its own.)

Combine in electric blender or food processor, using pulse control. It may be necessary to stop and push down material in blender. A processor creates a mixture with more texture than does a blender. Store in refrigerator, or in freezer for long term. Will keep 1 to 2 years in freezer.

Tips for Herbal Oil Concentrates

1. Remove woody stems from herbs; they may have a strong, bitter off-taste.

2. Cut chives (or green onions) into 1-inch pieces before blending so they will not wrap around blades.

3. For consistency, always measure herbs by firmly packing in container or by weighing.

4. Add parsley to strong-flavored herbs such as rosemary, winter savory, and thymes to smooth out flavor and to make up measurement for difficult-to-strip leaves. Recommended proportion is equal parts of parsley and other herb.

5. When preparing flavored oils, we always use dried chiles rather than fresh, so we do not have to worry about molding.

6. If you're freezing mixtures in glass containers,

leave ample headroom to allow for expansion. In fact, we prefer to leave the lid off the container until the mixture is frozen and we are sure that it doesn't expand past the top. Covered glass jars will break easily if overfilled.

7. Do not freeze mixtures which contain vinegar, citrus juice, or other acids. Store them in the refrigerator.

8. To guard against botulism, always freeze chopped or pureed garlic rather than just refrigerating.

9. As herbal oil concentrates are used, transfer the remainder to a smaller container to reduce the air space. (Containers should not be stored more than half empty.) The container may be lined with a plastic bag that is closed after each use, but this will complicate removal of the frozen mixture because of folds in the bag.

HERB HONEY

Herb honey is simple to make. It's best to use glass jars, and they must be scalded before use. When the containers are ready, wash, dry, and chop the fresh herbs of your choice, and add 2 to 5 tablespoons to a pint of any kind of honey. Delicately flavored rose petals and chamomile and lavender flowers can be used in larger quantities; strong herbs such as rosemary, anise, and the mints should be used more sparingly. Mix the herbs in thoroughly, then seal and label the jar and set it in a sunny place. After 5 to 10 days, strain out the herbs with a strainer or cheesecloth, rebottle, and the honey is ready to use. It's that easy!

Herb honey can replace white sugar in any recipe, with two adjustments: use only 1/3 to 1/2 as much honey as is called for in sugar, and reduce the other liquids in the recipe by up to 1/4 to compensate for the liquidity of the honey. In baked goods, you can add extra flour instead of reducing the liquids. Because honey-based baked goods brown faster than those made with sugar, it's also wise to reduce the oven temperature by about 25°F.

Herb Honey Jelly—*Makes four 6-ounce glasses*
If you like the flavor of honey but not its stickiness and runny consistency, try this recipe.

2 cups herb honey
3/4 cup water
1 bottle pectin

Follow the directions on the pectin bottle for making jelly with honey.

CRANBERRY-APPLE JELLY WITH ROSEMARY

Makes about 8 half-pints

This jelly is also very good made with thyme in place of the rosemary. Variations of this recipe can be prepared using apple or grape juice with rosemary or thyme. The cranberry-apple version is the prettiest— a bright, ruby-colored jelly with a green herb sprig. This is a soft jelly that is good served with all types of poultry, as a glaze for goose or duck, and with buttered toast or cream cheese and bagels.

If you are using sweetened cranberry-apple juice, use the lesser amount of sugar; if using natural-style cranberry-apple juice with no sweetener, add the extra cup of sugar.

6 cups cranberry-apple juice
5 3-inch sprigs rosemary or 6 to 7 3-inch sprigs thyme
5 to 6 cups sugar
1 box powdered pectin (1¼ or 2 ounces)
8 2-inch sprigs of rosemary or thyme, rinsed and patted dry

In a large, heavy-bottomed, noncorrodible pot, combine the juice and the larger herb sprigs. Bring to a boil, cover, remove from heat, and let stand for a least 20 minutes.

Remove the herb sprigs and stir in the pectin. Bring the juice to a boil, and stir at the boiling point for 1 minute. Add the sugar all at once and stir well. Bring to a boil that cannot be stirred down, and boil for 1 minute.

Place an herb sprig in each hot, sterilized, half-pint canning jar, and ladle in the hot jelly. Wipe the rims of the jars and seal immediately with hot, sterilized lids and rings. Place the jars on a heavy towel, and carefully invert them for 5 minutes. Turn the jars upright, cover with the towel, and cool to room temperature. Store any unsealed jars in the refrigerator, and use this jelly as soon as possible.

LAVENDER JELLY

5½ cups of apple juice
1½ cups fresh lavender blossoms
1 box of pectin
2 tablespoons lemon juice
7½ cups sugar

Wrap the blossoms loosely in cheesecloth. Combine blossoms and apple juice in a heavy sauce pan and bring to a boil. Remove from heat, let steep one hour, then remove blossoms. To avoid failure, add pectin, lemon juice, and sugar according to pectin package directions. Cook and seal according to instructions on the pectin package. To use as a salad dressing, stir one tablespoon of lavender jelly into cut-up fresh fruit. Chill and serve.

ZUCCHINI DILL PICKLES

Makes 4 pints

Small zucchini (about 1 inch in diameter) make the best pickles, but overgrown ones can make satisfactory pickles if they are halved, seeded, then cut into half-rings. Try to use the dill heads before they are completely mature and dry because of their soft flavor and appearance.

2 pounds small zucchini
2 medium onions
1/4 cup kosher salt
Ice water
2 cups cider vinegar
2 cups water
1 tablespoon sugar
1 tablespoon mustard seed
4 dill heads or 1/4 cup dill seed
4 or 5 garlic cloves, sliced thin
1 bunch dill leaves, large stems removed

Trim the ends from the zucchini and slice about 3/8 inch thick. Halve the onions lengthwise, then slice them crosswise about 1/4 inch thick. Layer the vegetables in a glass, ceramic, or stainless steel bowl, sprinkling each layer with salt. Cover with ice water. Place a plate on top of the vegetables and a weight on the plate. Let stand for 2 hours.

Drain the zucchini and onions and rinse well. Drain again while you prepare the pickling liquid.

Mix the vinegar, water, sugar, and mustard in a large nonreactive pan. Bring the mixture to a boil, then simmer for 5 minutes.

Remove the pan from the heat, add the dill heads or seed and the zucchini and onions, and cover. Let the mixture stand for 2 hours, tossing occasionally.

Meanwhile, fill a canning kettle with enough water to cover pint jars and bring the water to a boil. Sterilize four pint jars and scald four lids and rings.

Bring the zucchini mixture to a boil in its pan and stir in the garlic and dill leaves. Ladle into hot, sterilized pint jars. Cover with lids and rings and process in the boiling water bath according to manufacturer's directions for 10 minutes at sea level. Store the pickles for a week at room temperature before using. If any jars do not seal, store them in the refrigerator

and use the contents within 2 weeks.

Note: If you live 1000–3000 feet above sea level, increase the length of time in the boiling water bath by 5 minutes. Increase time by 10 minutes at 3000–6000 feet, 15 minutes at 6000–8000 feet, and 20 minutes above 8000 feet.

WHOLE-GRAIN MUSTARD

Makes about 1 cup

This flavorful, all-purpose mustard adds texture and tang to salad dressings and sandwiches.

1 tablespoon whole coriander seeds
6 tablespoons whole mustard seeds (a mixture of black and yellow)
1 tablespoon green peppercorns
1/2 teaspoon dried thyme
3/4 cup water
2 teaspoons honey
1/4 cup red wine vinegar

Toast coriander seeds in a dry skillet or place them in a flat dish and microwave on High for 4 to 5 minutes. Crush mustard seeds, green peppercorns, and coriander seeds in a mortar.

Mix the crushed seeds, thyme, and water in the upper pan of a glass, enamel, or stainless steel double boiler and let stand at least three hours.

Heat water to boiling in the lower pan of the double boiler. Reduce the heat to simmering and place the upper pan, containing the mustard mixture, on top. Stir in the honey and vinegar and cook 10 minutes until the mustard is as thick as you like. It will thicken a bit more as it cools. Refrigerate, covered.

JALAPEÑO MUSTARD

Makes about 1 pint

This mustard has just a bit of extra zip.

2 teaspoons whole coriander seeds
1/4 cup whole yellow mustard seeds
1/4 cup whole black mustard seeds
1/4 cup dry powdered mustard
3/4 cup cold water
3 cloves garlic, peeled and chopped
1 small onion, peeled and chopped
2 to 3 small jalapeño peppers, seeded
1/4 cup cider vinegar
1/4 cup dry white wine

Toast coriander seeds in a dry skillet or place them

CONDIMENTS &

A Leek Bouquet Garni, instructions opposite.

Bouquets Garnis

It's nice to have several different dry bouquets garnis on hand in the kitchen, ready to toss in the soup pot or add to a slow-simmering stew. Just mix your chosen herbs together in a small bowl and pack them into muslin or cheesecloth bouquet garni bags. Or place about a tablespoon of the mixed herbs on a 4-inch square of muslin or doubled cheesecloth and tie them up with unwaxed dental floss or lightweight kitchen string. An even more convenient way to package these is in empty tea bags. The tea-bag bouquet garni is a perfect size for preparing most dishes.

The best-known bouquet garni is made from parsley, sage, rosemary, and thyme. As dried parsley has little flavor, try adding fresh parsley to the dish, near the end of cooking, to retain the most flavor.

Mix your favorite herbs to make your own special blends. Using freshly dried herbs is most important. To avoid muddiness, don't use too many herbs. Use about a tablespoon of herb for each bouquet garni. The following simple combinations go well with most dishes.

in a flat dish and microwave on High for 4 to 5 minutes. Crush the mustard and coriander seeds slightly in a mortar or blender, then mix them and the powdered mustard into the water and let stand for at least three hours.

Mix the remaining ingredients and pulverize in a blender until smooth. Stir the puree into the mustard. Bring the mixture to a boil, then lower the heat and simmer 5 minutes or until as thick as you like, stirring occasionally. The mustard will thicken slightly on cooling. Refrigerate, covered.

BOUQUET GARNI

Mix together crumbled bay leaves, dried parsley, and dried thyme in these proportions: 1 bay leaf, 1 tablespoon parsley, 1 teaspoon thyme. Store in a covered jar, or make little muslin bags 2 inches square, placing a tablespoon of the mixture in each, to simmer in soups and stocks.

HEARTY BOUQUET GARNI

This heartier blend is good for stews, soups, meats, and other robust dishes.

Mix one part rosemary with one part thyme; add a little sage if you like. Pack the herbs into bouquet garni bags, adding a bay leaf and eight to ten peppercorns to each one.

SAVORY BOUQUET GARNI

This savory blend marries well with light soups and stews, stocks, and vegetable dishes.

Mix two parts marjoram with one part savory and one part thyme (optional). Toss the herbs gently in a small bowl to blend. Pack the herbs into bouquet garni bags with a bay leaf and a few peppercorns.

A LEEK BOUQUET GARNI

Instead of simply tying the twig ends of herbs together, you can wrap them in leek leaves, then tie the whole package. This is helpful when you want to add spices, aromatic herbs, or garlic to the bouquet.

Assemble the ingredients of your bouquet garni. Then wash two large green outer leaves from a leek, each about 10 inches long, and lay one, curved side up, on the table. Have ready a piece of strong cotton thread, kitchen twine, or unwaxed dental floss about 2 feet long. Place the herbs in the center of the leaf and fold the ends of the leek over so they meet in the middle. Wrap the other leek leaf, curved side down, over and around the folded leaf. Fold the ends of the second leaf over the back of the first. Tie the package as you would a roast: First, make a square knot at the center of one end of the package, leaving one end of the thread roughly twice as long as the other. Bring the long end down about an inch, then hold the thread in place with a finger while you wrap the free end under and around the package, perpendicular to the section of thread you are holding. Slip the free end of thread under the fixed section where your finger is holding it, and tighten. In the same way, bring the long end down another inch (to about the center), hold it, take another turn around the package, and bring the free end through. Tighten, then take one more turn around the package about an inch from the bottom. Finally, tie the loose ends together lengthwise.

HEARTY HERB BLEND

There's nothing tricky in this classic blend—you can multiply to your heart's content without worrying about proportions. Grind it fine and package in shaker bottles, or leave it coarse and pack in jars. It's good rubbed on roasts or added to hearty stews; forget the salt.

2 parts dried rosemary
2 parts dried savory
1 part dried thyme
1 part dried marjoram

TARRAGON MUSTARD

Makes about 3/4 cup

This sophisticated mustard is very simple to make.

1/4 cup black mustard seeds
1/4 cup yellow mustard seeds
1/4 cup dry powdered mustard
3/4 cup cold water
1/4 cup dry white wine
1/4 cup white wine vinegar
1 teaspoon dried tarragon
1/8 teaspoon ground allspice

Mix mustard seeds, powdered mustard, and water in the upper pan of a noncorrodible double boiler. Let stand at least three hours.

In another noncorrodible saucepan, mix the wine, vinegar, tarragon, and allspice and bring to a boil. Strain the liquid into the mustard mixture and blend well.

In the lower pan of the double boiler, heat water to boiling, then reduce heat to a simmer. Place the upper pan, containing the mustard mixture, on top. Cook, stirring, until the mustard is as thick as you like. It will thicken a bit more as it cools. Cover and refrigerate.

MULLING SPICE BEETLE

These make wonderful hostess or appreciation gifts, and are convenient to have on hand for brewing a tasty hot spiced cider. Here's all you need for one beetle:

1 orange
brown sugar
1 cinnamon stick
1 small whole nutmeg
2 whole allspice berries
6 to 8 whole cloves

Cut orange in half, juice it, and pull out any remaining pulp. Dry the shell in a low oven or microwave. When it's leathery-dry but not brittle, pack the shell with brown sugar, mounding it slightly. For the beetle's head, press the whole nutmeg halfway into the sugar near the edge of the shell. For the body, use a serrated knife to cut a piece of cinnamon stick 1 to 1½ inches long. Press it into the sugar. Add whole cloves on both sides of the cinnamon stick for legs, and the whole allspice berries for antennae.

For gift giving, wrap with plastic wrap and secure with a ribbon bow. Add a little card explaining to add the beetle to two quarts of apple cider and simmer for 30 minutes. For more "spice", add 1/4 to 1/2 cup brandy. Remove the spices and serve hot.

CANDIED FLOWERS

Gather fresh, perfect flowers. Rinse them carefully, pat dry, and place on paper towels.

Beat one egg white until frothy but not stiff. Dip each flower in egg white and shake gently to remove excess. Sprinkle white superfine granulated or confectioner's sugar all over the flower, coating the back as well as the front. Place on a shallow tray lined with waxed paper.

Dry in the refrigerator for one to two days. Store for as long as a month in airtight containers layered with waxed paper and placed in a cool, dry location.

Use to garnish cakes, ice cream, fruit salads, pies, and so on.

TO CRYSTALLIZE YOUR OWN GINGER

If you love crystallized ginger in steamed puddings, fruit salads, or ginger cookies, or dipped in bittersweet chocolate for an elegant treat, you might want to take the time to make your own. This recipe is easily doubled.

2 cups of 1/4-inch thick slices of peeled or scraped ginger
Water
1½ cups sugar
1/2 lemon, sliced
1 cup light corn syrup

First day: Cover ginger with water in a saucepan and bring slowly to a boil. Cover and simmer gently until tender, about 20 minutes. Add 1/2 cup sugar, stir well, and return to a boil. Remove from heat. Let stand, covered, at room temperature overnight.

Second day: Bring to a boil, reduce heat, and simmer gently for 15 minutes. Add sliced lemon and corn syrup. Simmer, uncovered, 15 minutes more, stirring occasionally. Remove from heat, cover, and let stand overnight.

Third day: Bring to a boil, stirring often. Stir in 1/2 cup sugar, bring to a boil, reduce heat, and simmer gently for 30 minutes. Stir in rest of sugar and bring to a boil. Remove from heat and let stand overnight.

Fourth day: Bring to a boil. When syrup drops heavily from the side of a spoon and the ginger is translucent, remove from heat and drain. Save syrup; it makes a delicious sauce. Dry ginger slices on a rack over a tray overnight. When well dried, roll in granulated sugar and store in tightly covered glass jars.

DELICIOUS POULTRY BLEND

Makes about 1 1/2 cups

All measurements are for firmly packed fresh herb leaves and tender stems.

1/2 cup parsley
1/2 cup garlic or onion chives, cut into 1-inch pieces
1/2 cup sweet marjoram or oregano
1/4 cup English or French thyme
1/4 cup garden sage
*4 fresh bay leaves, midribs removed, cut into 1/2-inch
   pieces*
1 tablespoon freshly ground coriander seed
1/2 cup vegetable oil

Combine all ingredients in processor or blender container. Blend until uniformly chopped. Store in freezer.

TOASTED CORIANDER SEEDS

Toasted and ground coriander seeds are a staple in many kitchens. Toast and grind about 1/2 ounce of seed at a time; prepare only as much as you'll use within two weeks.

To toast the seeds, place them in a small skillet over the lowest possible heat for just a minute or two, shaking the pan once or twice. They are done when you can just start to smell a coriander aroma. Don't brown them, or they will taste overtoasted and bitter. Remove the seeds from the heat and grind them with a spice grinder or mortar and pestle. Store the ground spice away from light and heat in a jar with a tight-fitting lid. The toasted seeds can be stored whole and ground as needed.

Index